Keep It Simple

FOR BUSY WOMEN

EMILIE BARNES

HARVEST HOUSE PUBLISHERS
Eugene, Oregon 97402

Cover by Terry Dugan Design, Bloomington, Minnesota

KEEP IT SIMPLE FOR BUSY WOMEN
Copyright © 2002 by Emilie Barnes
Published by Harvest House Publishers
Eugene, Oregon 97402

Library of Congress Cataloging-in-Publication Data
Barnes, Emilie.
    Keep it simple for busy women / Emilie Barnes
        p. cm.
    ISBN 0-7369-0553-7
    1. Women—Religious life.   2. Home economics.   I. Title.

BV4527 .B35876 2002
242'.643—dc21   2001051576

Printed in the United States of America.

    02 03 04 05 06 07 08 09 10 11 / BP-MS / 10 9 8 7 6 5 4 3 2

Contents

January

A WELL-DESIGNED LIFE

Begin with God

In the beginning was the Word, and the Word was with God, and the Word was God.

JOHN 1:1

Whether it's a project, a new day, a time set aside for being alone, or an important phone call, this bit of truth always applies: Begin with God!

If you want to be more organized and have more time to do the things that are important to you, start with God. After all, the Bible clearly tells us that our heavenly Father is the Alpha and the Omega—the beginning and the end. Let's start from there.

Today, as you work toward home organization, start by quieting your heart before Him. I've learned that when I have an "uncluttered heart" I have a lot better chance of establishing an uncluttered home.

Make sure everything has a designated place. One of my sayings is "Don't put it down, put it away." Get rid of all items you don't use. They just add to the clutter.

The missionary Hudson Taylor said, "Don't have your concert first and tune your instruments afterward." Begin with God. He'll lead you in the way you should go! He's good at that!

Simple Pleasures

- With snow falling outside, enjoy a steaming cup of hot chocolate.
- Reflect on the solitude of a winter garden.
- Open your windows and combine crisp air, a cozy throw, and a crackling fire.

Wisdom for Living

Here I am, Lord. Speak, and I will follow.

Creative Solutions

Being confident of this very thing, that he which hath begun a good work in you will perform it until the day of Jesus Christ.

PHILIPPIANS 1:6 (KJV)

Every day presents opportunities for growth. Every problem has a solution. Sometimes all it takes is to think a little differently than we have before.

Maybe your kitchen and dining room are combined offering you little privacy between the two. Consider installing a ceiling-hung venetian blind to separate the two areas. Trying to save money around the house? Cook as many foods in the oven at one time as you can...and on the stove top, match the size of the pan to the heating element so more heat will get to the pan.

Next time you crack one of your china cups, don't throw it out. Did you know that you can mend the crack in that cup—with milk? Immerse the cup in a pan of milk, simmer for three-quarters of an hour—then just wash and dry it. The protein in the milk is what works the miracle.

Speaking of milk, heed 1 Peter 2:2 (NASB): "Like newborn babies, long for the pure milk of the word, so that by it you may grow." Today let the Word of God dwell in your heart, and His creative heart will shape and mold yours. Growth is that simple!

Simple Pleasures

All the problems become smaller if you don't dodge them,
but confront them. Touch a thistle timidly, and it pricks you;
grasp it boldly, and its spines crumble.
—WILLIAM S. HALSEY

Wisdom for Living

*Dear Lord, thank You that You are committed to restoring me.
Make me whole. Begin today.*

Rewards for Cleaning House

> He that cometh to God must believe that he is, and that he is a rewarder of them that diligently seek him.
>
> HEBREWS 11:6 (KJV)

I'm a firm believer in rewards! And I reward myself often when it comes to some of the more mundane tasks of cleaning house. Discover your idea of bliss, and use it to make those tasks a little less mundane. Let me explain.

Cleaning house is a very personal issue. Start by not worrying about other people's standards. Decide what clean means to you, and make that your goal.

Establish simple, bite-size priorities. Identify those tasks that absolutely have to be done, ones that should be done, and ones that would be nice to get done. Work on them in that order—and forget the rest.

Set time limits. Do what you can now and be happy about it. Relish what you have accomplished instead of focusing on what still remains to be done. Finish one task before you begin another.

When you've finished, reward yourself for a job well-done. For me that often means a time of quiet—with my Bible, my journal, and a cup of tea—and my feet propped up. Discover your idea of bliss!

Simple Pleasures

- Experience a "lights out" night and live by candlelight.
- Share your favorite book with a friend and then find a quiet book shop to discuss your thoughts over coffee or tea.
- Settle into your favorite chair and breathe a sigh of relief.

Wisdom for Living

Lord, Your daily blessings fill my heart with such abundance.
May I pour out Your love on those around me.
Pleasing You is my highest reward.

Take Stock and Take Heart

*Commit thy works unto the Lord,
and thy thoughts shall be
established.*

PROVERBS 16:3 (KJV)

When was the last time you did something just for you? We all need periods of reappraisal and renewal. We all need time to take stock and take heart.

A quiet time gives us the opportunity to identify our most cherished goals and develop ways to achieve them. It also contributes to a sense of inner peace and makes us feel more in control of life.

How do you get started? Let me suggest some tools to help you. The first one is the Bible. Read it daily and say your prayers. Another helpful tool is to record your prayers, thoughts, and feelings in a journal.

Listen to good music while you write. Take that opportunity to turn off the TV. God wants to speak to our hearts.

Read a good book. Make activity dates for yourself and pencil them into your calendar. Make sure that you keep them.

Our crowded schedules and noisy world can make it difficult to take stock or take heart. And what do you do about the guilt of taking time for yourself? Get over it!

Simple Pleasures

Good books, like good friends,
are few and chosen; the more select,
the more enjoyable.
—LOUISA MAY ALCOTT

Wisdom for Living

*I want to think about You today, Lord. I want to bask in Your love and feel
Your acceptance all around me. Heart of mine, rest in your God.*

Celebrating Femininity

And he will be like a tree firmly planted by streams of water, Which yields its fruit in its season…and in whatever he does, he prospers.

PSALM 1:3 (NASB)

We may never look like models or movie stars, but we can honor God's gift of femininity by taking care of the unique person He created you and me to be.

My daily walks help me keep my figure under control. I look forward to how wonderful I feel after this brisk morning exercise. It always restores my energy, lifts my spirits, and gives me a sense of well-being that makes it easier for me to reach out to others. Yet, as much as I believe in taking care of myself, that's not enough.

True beauty comes from within. If that beauty is lacking, no exercise program, eating plan, or wardrobe update can put it there. No interior decorating scheme can give it to me. First Peter 3:4 defines it wonderfully by telling us that, "the unfading beauty of a gentle and quiet spirit…is of great worth in God's sight."

Today, take a few moments to reflect on the grace and peace that God offers you every day. Spend 15 minutes reading God's Word and allow His Spirit to focus your heart and mind and create in you a gentle, quiet spirit. Today, seek the beauty that comes from within. It's as simple as that.

Simple Pleasures

- Write your notes with a feathered pen. It's so elegant!
- Pin a silk flower on your lapel or add it to your hair.
- Create a parlor look with stacks of books and warm fabrics.

Wisdom for Living

I want my roots to go down deeply into Your love today, dear Jesus. Nurture and nourish me. Revive my soul so that I may serve You with a perfect heart.

The New Has Come

Sing unto him a new song; play skilfully with a loud noise. For the word of the Lord is right; and all his works are done in truth.

PSALM 33:3-4 (KJV)

If your house is bursting at the seams with small children, and chaos is nipping at your heels...

If your nest is empty and your steps echo in the silence...

If your career or your relationships seem to be falling apart...

The spirit of godliness can help your feet find the right path.

Inner peace, strength, confidence, and tranquillity come from depending on God. They come from obeying Him, drawing on His strength and wisdom, and learning to be like Him. After all, our identity can only be found in Him. When this happens, we know how much we are worth in God's sight. Becoming a woman of God begins with making a personal commitment to Jesus Christ. Second Corinthians 5:17 says, "If anyone is in Christ, he is a new creation; the old has gone, the new has come!" What a simply wonderful gift!

No matter what you are facing today, trust the simplicity of God's promise through Christ. Trust Him to create a new day for you in every area of your life.

Simple Pleasures

- Start a garden club, a book club, or an investment club with friends.
- Volunteer at the local library or your neighborhood school.
- Take a walk around your block and smile at those you meet.

Wisdom for Living

I am trusting You for a new season in my life. I am ready to begin again and I need You, dear heavenly Father, to show me the way.

Who's on the Throne?

Where were you when I laid the earth's foundation? Tell me, if you understand.

JOB 38:4

Who's in control of your life? Who's ruling and reigning from the command center? Where no plan is laid, chaos will soon reign! Here's how to start to bring calm to the clutter and order to the disorderliness.

You're going to need four basic tools: the first is a To Do list. Write down all the things that you need to do today and in the short term. Then mark them off as they're completed.

Second, get a calendar. In fact, get several of them—a month-at-a-glance, a week-at-a-glance for more details, and another that has a page for an entire day.

Third, you'll need a telephone/address/e-mail source list for all those important numbers you need to keep handy.

And finally, set up a simple filing system with this motto in mind: "Don't pile it, file it!" Don't you feel better already?

Now take some time to thank the Lord for all He's done for you and for His faithfulness in your life! We worship the God who set the stars in the heavens!

Simple Pleasures

- Curl up with a quilt and watch your favorite weekly program.
- Turn off the television and listen to music all week long.
- Do something unpredictable tonight.

Wisdom for Living

*I understand so little, Lord, of what you are trying to accomplish
or of how You work Your will. But I know You love me,
and today, that's all I need to know.*

Leaving a Legacy

> Be thou diligent to know the state of thy flocks, and look well to thy herds. For riches are not for ever: and doth the crown endure to every generation?
>
> PROVERBS 27:23-24 (KJV)

What kind of legacy are you going to leave your heirs? It's exciting to realize that you will leave something behind, even if it's only in the way people remember you. Let's talk for a moment about your legacy.

In 2 Timothy 1:5 (NASB) we see a legacy in action when Paul says, "I am mindful of the sincere faith within you, which first dwelt in your grandmother Lois, and your mother Eunice—and I am sure that it is in you as well." It's easy to think of a legacy in terms of financial resources or material possessions. But have you ever considered the value of leaving behind the qualities of faith, hope, and love to those who love and cherish you?

You and I have the incredible opportunity to leave behind a legacy—one of care and concern, one that reaches out to others, one of loveliness and holiness. Be a mom who cares about the kind of legacy you leave when the Lord calls you home. Follow God's plan for you. Pattern your life from what you've learned. And simply pass it on to those who will follow.

Simple Pleasures

- Savor your town and taste all its seasons.
- Polish up a crisp apple and enjoy it with a special cheese.
- Decorate an antique table with a pretty basket filled with home-made muffins.

Wisdom for Living

Heavenly Father, thank You for the responsibilities I face today. I need Your grace to walk faithfully through this day. I want my life to be a godly witness, Lord, for today and the days to come.

Live in the Present

For he is our God and we are the people of his pasture, the flock under his care.

PSALM 95:7

Today—just live for today. No regrets for the past. No worries about tomorrow. No thoughts about future "maybes!"

As you do, you'll discover something quite amazing: You'll find yourself smiling again. You'll find it easier to laugh. Your prayers will be more about praise and less about petition. You'll even find it easier to think! Your mind won't be cluttered with things that have already happened and thoughts about what might never come to pass. In short, you'll be enjoying what the moment brings.

Often our greatest anxieties are about things we have no control over. Eighty-five percent of the things we worry about never happen! Why do we spend so much time and energy on something that probably won't occur?

Just for today, stop and smell the roses, hear the train whistle, see the puffy clouds in the sky, and enjoy life as God has given it to us. When we begin to see and experience the "minute," we will begin to see the grandeur of God—and His goodness.

Simple Pleasures

- Run a hot bath, light a candle, and soak away your cares.
- Pick up a few favorite magazines at the store—treat yourself.
- The smell of hot apple pie is worth a lot!

Wisdom for Living

Soften my heart, Lord. There is so much that has the power to distract and tempt me. Keep me soft toward You.

Wrapping Our Lives in Cloth

> *But put on the Lord Jesus Christ, and make no provision for the flesh in regard to its lusts.*
>
> ROMANS 13:14 (NASB)

If you need tips for using fabric in decorating your home, wait no more! And—trust me—I'm going to keep it simple!

Whenever you see a length of cute, inexpensive fabric, snap it up. You will be surprised at all the uses you'll find for it. For example, wrap a present using a glue gun and fabric ribbon. Disguise an ugly lamp. Set the lamp on a large circle of fabric and bring up the fabric like a pouch—tie just under the shade with ribbon and it's as good as new! Use fabric to brighten your home and give it a unique look.

Let's think a little more deeply about what "covering" can mean in our lives. In Luke 2:12-14 (NASB), the angel declares: "'This will be a sign for you: you will find a baby wrapped in cloths and lying in a manger.' And suddenly there appeared…a multitude of the heavenly host praising God and saying, 'Glory to God in the Highest!'"

God has wrapped us in His love and care. He has covered our sins with the blood of His Son Jesus. Most amazing of all, He has clothed us in the robes of righteousness and called us His "chosen ones." What a blessing He is!

Simple Pleasures

- Capture favorite quotations or thoughts in a personal journal.
- Cover your journal with a beautiful piece of cloth.
- Find a moment every week to think on these great thoughts.

Wisdom for Living

You are the Prince of Peace, and You have called me Your friend, Your dearly beloved, Your "chosen one." Jesus, I worship You.

The Lost Art of Eating Together

Listen, listen to me, and eat what is good, and your soul will delight in the richest of fare.

ISAIAH 55:2

Don't let our modern culture take away some of the most precious times you can have as a family. One of those is sharing a meal together sometime during the day. Here are some ideas on how to keep it simple.

Pick at least one meal of the day when your chances for getting everyone around the table are best. If one meal each day is too demanding, compromise. Set a goal of eating as a family four days a week instead of seven.

Involve your children in planning and cooking those special meals. Preparing foods in a different way can capture kids' interest. Use pasta in unusual shapes. Draw a smiling face on top of a casserole with cheese or veggie strips. Make it a time of fun and fellowship. Even teenagers should be involved in meal preparation. It can be an important time for conversation and interaction.

Then, when it's time to eat, don't forget to offer a prayer of thanksgiving. Model a heart of gratitude, peace, and warmth around your table. Now, relax and enjoy the meal. Great memories can come from these daily times of sharing!

Simple Pleasures

The bird a nest, the spider a web, me a friendship…

—WILLIAM BLAKE

Wisdom for Living

Slow me down, Lord. I want to be available for the minute conversation, or the gentle hug, or the quick smile. Don't let me miss those important opportunities to bless those I love.

The Wisdom of Living Wisely

For the Lord gives wisdom; from His mouth come knowledge and understanding.

PROVERBS 2:6 (NASB)

Life can get pretty crazy, can't it? We live in a day when people have put God on hold. The attitude that "I can do it myself, I don't need help from anyone!" is one of the most prevalent in our society. And we especially don't need help from a God we can't even see.

Recently I saw a great saying that read, "What the fool does at the end, wise men do at the beginning." Keeping your life simple is all about redeeming the time. About not spinning your wheels. About having your steps ordered by the Lord. But how can we do that when the world tells us to go it alone?

How different is the counsel God's Word gives us about avoiding a wasted life! Psalm 111:10 (NASB) says, "The fear of the Lord is the beginning of wisdom; a good understanding have all those who do His commandments. His praise endures forever."

If you want your life to count—for eternity—as a wife, a mom, or a single woman, the advice is the same! Go to the cross of Jesus and trust Him for wisdom.

Simple Pleasures

Wisdom is not finally tested in the schools,
Wisdom cannot be passed from one having it
 to another not having it,
Wisdom is of the soul, is not susceptible of proof,
 is its own proof.

—WALT WHITMAN

Wisdom for Living

I am humbly before You, Lord, at the foot of Your cross. Show me the way.

When my anxious thoughts multiply within me, Thy consolations delight my soul.

PSALM 94:19 (NASB)

Are you overwhelmed today by all the projects you feel you must accomplish? Do you find yourself on a treadmill of one thing after another, until you feel you'll never get off?

How can you have time for the important things you want to do, like prayer time, Bible study, reading to your kids, or making a special batch of cookies for your family? Well, you can do it all, but it will take some planning.

First, be ruthless—get rid of extra paper! Almost 90 percent of the paper in your home (or office) is never referred to again. Get rid of it!

And then apply this simple rule, which I call the "five-minute pickup" rule. Pick up and dust each room for five minutes—time yourself with a kitchen timer! Discipline yourself to stop when the bell goes off.

Sometimes all it takes to eliminate mess, clutter, and confusion are a few hooks here, a basket or two there, and a bit of reshuffling of items on a shelf. Give it a try and make your life a lot simpler!

Simple Pleasures

I avoid looking forward or backward,
and try to keep looking upward.

—CHARLOTTE BRONTE

Wisdom for Living

Oh, just to rest in Your presence for a moment or two. So many things to do, places to be. I want to be with You in it all, dear Lord.
Come—I welcome Your presence.

Don't Be Intimidated!

Let us therefore come boldly unto the throne of grace, that we may obtain mercy, and find grace to help in time of need.

I've heard it a million times, expressed with admiration and usually a little envy, "Oh, she's so creative." Usually it describes an "artsy" kind of person—someone who paints or writes or makes pottery. But some of us have even been a bit jealous of the friend who simply knows how to put a room together or combine fabrics in a way that is especially attractive. It's so easy to lose our confidence—if we ever had it to begin with.

Today, refuse to be intimidated by your own insecurities. Be bold! You really don't have to be an artist to infuse your home—and life—with the spirit of creativity.

Creativity is a God-given ability to take something ordinary and make it into something special! It's an openness to doing old things in new ways! And you are just as creative as the next person! Most of us just keep it hidden.

The creative spirit is part of our heritage as children of the One who created all things. And nurturing our creativity is part of our responsibility as stewards of God's good gifts.

Simple Pleasures

- Find some roses today. Buy one for yourself and one for someone you love.
- A fragrance spray can enliven any room in your house.
- Draw a picture and mail it to a child with your words of encouragement.

Wisdom for Living

Overcome my fears, Lord, as I cast them upon You.
Make me strong and courageous to show forth Your love.

19

The Gift of Trust

My God, my rock, in whom I take
refuge;
My shield and the horn of my
salvation, my stronghold and my
refuge;
My savior, Thou dost save me
from violence.

2 SAMUEL 22:3-4 (NASB)

Real trust is a gift you give to someone you love!

For many years, I've had tea parties with my granddaughter, Christine. I trusted her to drink very carefully out of my delicate china teacups. I knew she could easily break them, but I took that risk to show her how special she was to me. And she got the message!

This wonderful ritual I share with my granddaughter has given me a little insight into how God fills my cup with trust.

This most trustworthy God teaches me to trust—by trusting me! It's simple, but oh, so profound. More and more, as I grow older, I've become aware of God's love and trust working in my life.

He allows the pain and the fear I often experience, because He trusts me to respond in a way that will allow me to grow through them rather than be discouraged by them. And as I surrender my heart to trust Him, I hear Him say, "Go ahead, You can trust Me." And I've found that I truly can!

Simple Pleasures

- Begin collecting lovely toiletries—powders, unguents, creams.
- Start an evening ritual of herbal tea and a candle. Nourish a sense of calm.
- Pretty new pillowcases add a special touch to old, familiar sheets.

Wisdom for Living

*I trust You, Lord. I trust You with my yesterdays,
my todays, and all my tomorrows.*

Now That's Creative!

> *For by him were all things created, that are in heaven, and that are in earth, visible and invisible, whether they be thrones, or dominions, or principalities, or powers: all things were created by him, and for him.*

COLOSSIANS 1:16 (KJV)

Creativity keeps life interesting and fun. It also demonstrates that we are enthusiastic about the people and projects in our lives. Creativity is one of the qualities of our Creator-God. Start by believing that you are creative—and then look for ways to express that creativity today.

Use your imagination to display your fine collection of cups and saucers, bells, dolls, Hummels, or salt-and-pepper shakers. If this collection brings you pleasure, it will also be a blessing to friends and family around you.

A friend of mine displayed her collection of teddy bears in a clean but nonfunctional fireplace. Now that's creative! Another woman I know collects photographs of the people she loves. She put track lighting down a long, dark hallway and displayed over 30 photographs of family and friends in an assortment of pretty frames. Now *that's* creative!

Take a moment to change a room setting, rearrange a bookshelf, or place a vase of flowers somewhere new or unique. It doesn't need to be fancy to be creative!

Simple Pleasures

From fairest creatures
we desire increase,
That thereby beauty's rose
might never die.

—WILLIAM SHAKESPEARE

Wisdom for Living

*O God, Your creativity is beyond my comprehension.
Every day Your mercies are new. Today, I open my heart
to Your newness, to Your mercies, to Your love.*

The Five-Minute Miracle

The Sabbath was made for man, not man for the Sabbath.

MARK 2:27

If you're going to have time for the important things, then you need to have the five-minute principle well in place in your thinking. It means not letting those five-minute segments slip away just because you think they aren't long enough to get anything important done. Remember that most small chores can be accomplished in bits and pieces of time.

In just five minutes, you can make an appointment, file your nails, water houseplants, make out a party guest list, order tickets for a ball game, or sew a button on.

If you have ten minutes, you can write a short letter or note, pick out a birthday card, repot a plant, straighten your desktop, or exercise.

You get the idea—do small chores that occupy little time. But don't overdo it. Leave some slack in your day for God's little surprises. Who knows, maybe today the Lord will give you the opportunity to have a small talk with a neighbor, to enjoy a few minutes with a child over cookies and milk, or to make a quick visit to drop off a bouquet of flowers. Let your life be full of five-minute miracles.

Simple Pleasures

* "Do it now."
* Try putting a bunch of flowers in your refrigerator. Beautiful!
* Purchase several birthday cards all at once so that you will be ready throughout the year.

Wisdom for Living

Gracious Father, I sometimes underestimate what You can do in my heart in just a moment. As I rest in You, show me how to make the most of the moments You are giving me.

The Beauty of "Real"

When he appears, we shall be like him, for we shall see him as he is.

1 JOHN 3:2

Do you remember the beautiful little story of *The Velveteen Rabbit?* You've probably read it to your children.

It's the story of a stuffed rabbit who wanted to be real. It took a long time to be given the gift of "real." But this bunny was so loved by his young owner that when his fur was worn and his face was gone and his stuffing had come out, he finally became "real."

The Velveteen Rabbit wasn't a patched up bunny—he was a beautiful, real rabbit, set free by love. That's the kind of healing I look forward to eventually—a healing that's full and complete.

When God is through with us, we will be more "real" than we ever thought possible—a bit scarred and a bit wrinkled, but full of energy and life and love.

It's quite a process, becoming real. But what could be more important? I think that the men and women who become real are those that truly look like the Lord Jesus Christ. I don't know about you, but I just can't wait!

Simple Pleasures

To improve the golden moment of opportunity and catch the good that is within our reach is the great art of life.

—WILLIAM JAMES

Wisdom for Living

Lord, my heart's desire is to be like You.

The Spirit of Loveliness

Then the righteous will shine like the sun in the kingdom of their Father.

As godly women, we have the wonderful opportunity to let our lives sparkle with God's love!

I thought you might like to know of some "sparklers" you can use to complete the spirit of loveliness in your life!

Frame a card with your favorite Scripture verse and hang it next to your desk or sink.

Put a family photo in your bathroom in an attractive frame. Pray each morning for those you love while you're brushing your teeth, doing your makeup, or fixing your hair.

Make sure your kids have a good children's Bible. Read aloud to them during your time together.

Be on the lookout for ways to obey God by serving others.

It's simple to turn your everyday activities into occasions for prayer and thanksgiving!

Simple Pleasures

- New kitchen dishtowels will brighten the "heart of the home."
- Grate fresh parmesan cheese on a crisp green salad.
- Bake chocolate chip cookies and let the smell say "welcome home."

Wisdom for Living

Shine through me this day, Lord. Shine Your righteousness, Your strength, and Your truth to all those around me. Shine, Jesus, shine.

Expressions of Love

> But godliness with contentment is
> great gain.
>
> 1 TIMOTHY 6:6

As a child bride of 17, I began my decorating journey with almost nothing. In those days I was trying to create a beautiful home on no budget at all! My husband, Bob, and I spray painted an old wrought-iron garden table for our kitchen. We rooted around behind charity shops for interesting discards, and we even moved our little plants from room to room, just for some variety.

Without knowing it, we were learning a lot about what we love, and how we can share ourselves by sharing our home. We also fell more in love with each other as we spent time creating our home.

It wasn't always easy, though. Sometimes we had to work a bit to marry Bob's tastes with mine, but we kept working at it, and it's been well worth it! Even today, our home is an ongoing creation—an expression of our love.

You don't know what the future may hold, so practice the art of contentment. What we have right now is this one day. May God give us a peace of mind that lets us rest—right where He's placed us!

Simple Pleasures

- Embark on a spontaneous midnight walk and do some stargazing.
- Take advantage of sales to add to your candle supply.
- Wake your spouse early and enjoy a moment of prayer together.

Wisdom for Living

Heavenly Father, You know the beginning from the end.
I place my hope in You today. I know I can never be
disappointed by Your love or Your plans for me!

The Joy of Two Homes

One thing I ask of the Lord, this is what I seek: that I may dwell in the house of the Lord all the days of my life, to gaze upon the beauty of the Lord and to seek him in his temple.

PSALM 27:4

Consider making two homes for yourself—one actual home, and a second spiritual home. Establish and create a "home to come home to," but nurture your spiritual home—and carry it with you always! Today, let's talk about storage! It's an important word in organizing both homes.

Storing things around the house is a real headache, so let's get started. A garage-sale wine rack or a wire bike basket attached to the wall are perfect for towels! You know the baskets you've been saving? Hang them on a wall for your napkins or table linens. An old set of drawers is great for holding videotapes or CDs.

Pick up an unfinished toy box and paint it in adult colors. It doubles as a lamp table and lots of storage! I love to use cardboard boxes for everything and anything! Use spray adhesive to cover a cardboard box with fabric; add some trim and use it in any room of your house.

And while you're busy around the house, tack up a few notecards with verses on them and do a little storing of God's Word!

Simple Pleasures

* Memorize an inspiring poem or favorite section of Scripture.
* Clip articles from magazines and create a reading file.
* A pretty apron can make your evening chores a little more inviting.

Wisdom for Living

Lord, help me to set my affections on things above. Help me to seek Your kingdom first. I want my life to reflect Your presence, Lord.

February

No Better Time

The Sweet Savor

*So teach us to number our days,
that we may apply our hearts unto
wisdom.*

PSALM 90:12 (KJV)

Why bother with any of those around-the-house tips? Here's why: Organization and efficiency can give us more time to pursue the things that really matter. Try some of these ideas over the next few days. They really work!

Do you seem to never have enough lemon juice when you need it? Squeeze the juice of fresh lemons into ice cube trays. Then just defrost them and use them when you're ready. It's wonderful having fresh lemon juice at your fingertips!

Do you spend precious minutes scrubbing pots and pans with burned-on food? Drop one or two fabric-softener sheets into the water. Let it stand for an hour or so and the food will lift right off.

Keep your kitchen smelling fresh and sweet by washing your sink with a strong salt solution or even with laundry bleach.

Creating a home filled with order and cleanliness communicates a heart that is ordered and pure. Take a moment today to make your home more simply organized and see how the sweet savor blesses those around you.

Simple Pleasures

- Puttering is acceptable. Enjoy your home, and don't always be on task.
- A cup of hot broth is a comforting beverage this time of year.
- Frame a card from a loved one—let it be a "grace note" in your home.

Wisdom for Living

*O God, I long for a pure heart, for I know You are pure.
Purify me by Your Spirit and I will be pure.*

Cluttered Closet, Cluttered Mind

Thy word have I hid in mine heart, that I might not sin against thee.

PSALM 119:11 (KJV)

What's in that closet of yours? Maybe it's been quite some time since you really looked. Your closet is full and "you don't have a thing to wear." Sound familiar? It's time for a major reconstruction job.

Take everything out of the closet. If you haven't worn something for a year, consider getting rid of it. Hang clothes in categories. Put your belts and scarves where you can see them. Pick up a wardrobe organizer at a local discount store. Put your shoes on a shoe rack at the bottom of the closet.

After you've sorted it all out, you have only three options: give away, throw away, or put away! What a boost it will give you to take the time to get organized.

In a quiet moment, think about your "inner closet." Is it clean and well organized too? Do a little inner closet cleaning today. Give away a kind word for someone dear, throw away painful memories, and put away the Word of God in your heart to serve you in the seasons of life that lie ahead.

Simple Pleasures

We only need one set of roots. Living takes time.

—ELEANOR BROWN

Wisdom for Living

Search me today, O Lord, and shine Your holy light on anything that needs to be removed from my life or set right again. I trust You, Lord, to show me.

The Real Treasure of Man

A man's life does not consist in the abundance of his possessions.

Luke 12:15

I love this poem by Edgar Guest. Keep it simple today, won't you?

The Simple Things

I would not be too wise—so very wise
   That I must sneer at simple songs and creeds,
And let the glare of wisdom blind my eyes
   To humble people and their humble needs.

I would not care to climb so high that I
   Could never hear the children at their play,
Could only see the people passing by,
   And never hear the cheering words they say...

God grant that I may live upon this earth
   And face the tasks which every morning brings
And never lose the glory and the worth
   Of humble service and the simple things.

—Edgar Guest

Simple Pleasures

* Select a pretty basket for mail. Make opening your mail a relaxing ritual.
* Be a bit early for your next appointment—take the moments to rest.
* Take a few moments to focus on your breathing. You'll feel renewed.

Wisdom for Living

The time You give me is one of Your most precious gifts, Lord.
May I learn to enjoy each moment and live it to the fullest!
Someday, I will be with You in eternity!

The Beauty of a Grateful Heart

For thou, Lord, hast made me glad through thy work: I will triumph in the works of thy hands. O Lord, how great are thy works! and thy thoughts are very deep.

PSALM 92:4-5 (KJV)

Is there anything more beautiful to God or others than a person with a grateful heart? Practice developing a grateful heart today by directing your spirit toward the beauty of God's creation. Here are some ideas to get you started.

Go outside regardless of the weather. Bundle up if it's cold. Take an umbrella for rain or put on shorts for a sunny summer day. Look around and take specific note of the beauty created by God for you to enjoy. You may see mist over a pond, red tomatoes on a green vine, sparkles of white snow in the sun, or your child's face. Beauty is there...and it's God's gift to you. Let it refresh and restore you. Remember, it's the simple things that make life enjoyable.

As you reflect on the bounty of beauty that surrounds you every day, say a prayer to the Creator and thank Him for placing you in such a beautiful world.

Simple Pleasures

- Take an afternoon and visit your local museum.
- Grab a friend and catch the afternoon matinee. Splurge on popcorn.
- Write down your dreams in your journal. These are the riches of life.

Wisdom for Living

Dear Lord, help me to see Your beauty today in all that is around me. May my gratitude spill over from a cup full of thanks to You.

An Atmosphere of Love

And walk in love, as Christ also hath loved us, and hath given himself for us an offering and a sacrifice to God for a sweetsmelling savour.

EPHESIANS 5:2 (KJV)

I'll never forget my excitement more than 40 years ago when my husband, Bob, carried me over the threshold of our first apartment. It had three tiny rooms and very little furniture, but it felt like a castle to us. We were so proud of that first home, a place to nurture our love and to begin our life together.

We wanted to create an atmosphere steeped in the joy of the Lord. We wanted to share God's blessings with everyone who entered, to embrace and draw them into God's love.

So we began by putting our hearts and souls into the simple things around us. We had one canvas chair, a box for a lamp table, and an old trunk for a coffee table. But it was enough. Out of that simple, humble beginning came wonderful relationships and the beginning of our life of ministry together.

God doesn't need extravagant beginnings to create extraordinary ends. Just look at Bethlehem and the manger. Use what God has given you to bless the lives of others, starting today.

Simple Pleasures

I dwell in possibility.

—EMILY DICKINSON

Wisdom for Living

You love simple things, Father—the simple truth, simple honesty, simple beginnings. Teach me to value simplicity and to seek it.

Sticking Close

For as the body is one, and hath many members, and all the members of that one body, being many, are one body: so also is Christ.

1 CORINTHIANS 12:12 (KJV)

I'm convinced that a godly life was never meant to be lived in a vacuum. It's really quite simple when you think about it.

The New Testament makes it clear that Christ's people are meant to function as a body—praying together, enjoying one another, working to do God's business in the world. How can we do this in the busy, pressured world in which we live?

Being involved in a vital, Bible-centered church is one way I stay close to the body of Christ. If work keeps you away on Sunday, try finding a small Bible study that fits your schedule at another time during the week.

Some of my most precious moments of Christian fellowship have happened within my own family—times of sharing with Bob over breakfast, sweet times of prayer as I tucked a child into bed. It's during these intimate moments that we really get down to business in our lives—loving, encouraging, and holding each other accountable for our growth in Christ.

Stick close to the those God has placed in your life. They are His gift to you!

Simple Pleasures

- A vase of flowers on your desk will brighten your day!
- Rituals are anchors for our lives.
- Lunchtime is a moment to step outside and breathe deeply of fresh air.

Wisdom for Living

How I long for closeness—to know and be known. Open my heart and life to others, dear Jesus. I want to be like You—loving and kind and open.

Me, Get Organized?

For I will set mine eyes upon them for good, and I will bring them again to this land: and I will build them, and not pull them down; and I will plant them, and not pluck them up.

What is it that causes you to be disorganized? And really, what difference does it make anyway? The answer to both those questions is found in understanding a God who values order and simplicity. Look around at the universe and you will find an amazingly ordered and efficient world. Here are a few ideas for organizing your life. The first one is to keep it simple!

The word "organized" means many things to many people. For some, it's putting papers in colored file folders. For others, it means putting all their seasonings on a shelf in alphabetical order. For some it means a clean house, and for others, being able to retrieve papers that have been stored.

Even after writing many books on the subject, I'm not sure I've covered all the bases for all women. I have found that it "starts with you"! Organized people have a calmness and serenity about them that disorganized people don't have. Search yourself to see what's causing all that confusion. And get rid of the clutter before you move on! What is it the Scripture says? "Everything should be done in a fitting and orderly way" (1 Corinthians 14:40).

Simple Pleasures

- A new nightgown or pajamas can make you feel like you're on vacation.
- Notice design details and adapt them to your home.
- Use a crystal glass for your morning juice. It's a touch of elegance.

Wisdom for Living

The greatest thing in all my life is knowing You.

Emilie's Top Ten List

Then we which are alive and remain shall be caught up together with them in the clouds, to meet the Lord in the air: and so shall we ever be with the Lord.

1 THESSALONIANS 4:17 (KJV)

Through the years, I've collected hundreds of helpful hints to make your home and your life more organized so that you have time for the really significant things God has gifted you to do. This is my Top Ten List. Here goes!

- Group your shopping trips together. Plan your errands.
- Purchase more than one like item of things you use often.
- Plan on doing more than one thing at a time.
- Use your body clock to do difficult things when your mind is sharpest.
- Always store your keys and glasses in the same place.
- Have your purchases picked up and delivered. More and more companies are offering these services, so use them!
- Become a list maker.
- Stop procrastinating. Start that engine of yours and get in motion.
- It doesn't have to be perfect.
- And above all, keep it simple!

Simple Pleasures

Tell me what you like, and I'll tell you what you are.

—JOHN RUSKIN

Wisdom for Living

*You're coming back someday, Jesus, to take me home.
Until that day, each day is a gift. Help me to live
to the fullest—full of grace, peace, forgiveness, love.*

Power of Prayer

O Lord, open my lips,
and my mouth will declare
your praise.

PSALM 51:15

This is a poem to help you *keep it simple* today.

The Difference

I got up early one morning and rushed into the day;
I had so much to accomplish that I didn't have time to pray.
Problems tumbled about me, and heavier came each task.
"Why doesn't God help me?" I wondered. He answered, "You
  didn't ask."
I wanted to see joy and beauty, but the day was gray and bleak;
I wondered why God didn't show me. He said, "But you didn't seek."
I tried to come into God's presence; I used all my keys at the lock.
God gently and lovingly chided, "My child, you didn't knock."
I woke up early this morning, and paused before entering the day.
I had so much to accomplish that I had to take time to pray.

—GRACE L. NAESSENS

Dear friend, keep your life simple before Him, won't you?

Simple Pleasures

- Send a psalm to a loved one and tell them you prayed for them today.
- Be flexible. It's one of the greatest gifts we have.
- "And what he greatly thought, he nobly dared."

—HOMER

Wisdom for Living

I lift my prayers to You, O God. I know You are ever with me.
Today, I will live my life before You and seek to do Your will.

The Tyranny of the Urgent

Call unto me, and I will answer thee, and shew thee great and mighty things, which thou knowest not.

JEREMIAH 33:3 (KJV)

Are you doing what's important in your day—or only what's urgent? Oftentimes what seems urgent isn't as important as something else we could be doing. How do we sort this out with the press of activities, daily demands, a job, and family obligations? Have you considered that the fruit that comes from spending time with your heavenly Father might be the answer?

In Galatians 5, Paul writes, "The fruit of the Spirit is love, joy, peace, patience, kindness, goodness, faithfulness, gentleness, self-control."

"But," you say, "who has time? My To Do list is always longer than my day. How can I possibly find time to do one more thing?"

We all make choices. And when we don't make time for God in our day—when we don't make time for the most important relationship in our life—we're probably not making the best choices!

Time with your heavenly Father is never wasted. Spend time alone with God each day. You'll walk through your day refreshed and ready for whatever comes your way!

Simple Pleasures

- Catalogs can be wonderful inspirations for decorating ideas.
- Take an hour to brew up a cup of tea and browse those catalogs.
- Make a simple purchase that will add to the comfort of your home.

Wisdom for Living

Your insights and revelations nourish my soul. Speak to me today, Lord. I long to hear Your call and obey Your voice.

The Miracle of Morning

Are you rushing around, never completing any one job? And when you do, is there a little one behind you, messing everything up again? Life can be more simple than that!

Years ago, I read in Proverbs 3:6 (NASB): "In all your ways acknowledge Him, and He will make your paths straight." I fell to my knees, "Please, God, direct my path—I'm tired!" The Lord heard my prayer that day and He honored it as well.

I began committing 15 minutes a day to my quiet time with the Lord. But even that was difficult to do, until I discovered the secret of getting up 15 minutes earlier than the rest of the family. The only way for me to ensure a quiet 15 minutes on a consistent basis in my busy household was to find that time early in the morning.

The house was wonderfully quiet, and my Lord and I talked as I read His Word and prayed. The Lord redeemed my time with Him. I had more time to plan meals, play with the children, and even catch a nap from time to time. God promises, "I will direct your path!"

Simple Pleasures

Prayer at its highest is a two-way conversation—and for me
the most important part is listening to God's reply.

—FRANK C. LAUBACH

Wisdom for Living

Be still, my soul. The Lord is on your side!

38

Preparation Is Everything

If ye do return unto the Lord with all your hearts…and prepare your hearts unto the Lord, and serve him only: and he will deliver you out of the hand of the Philistines.

1 SAMUEL 7:3 (KJV)

The Bible wisely instructs us to count the cost before we begin a project. That is good advice, especially in the kitchen. Here are five cooking tips that will make a difference!

Take out all your ingredients at the beginning of a cooking project. This will help assure you have everything you need before you start. As you use the ingredients, put them away! The cleanup is easier and there's no doubt whether or not you've used an ingredient.

When you're running short on time, reach for your favorite recipes on the inside of your kitchen cabinet doors. If you'll tape them there, you won't be scrambling to find the recipe the next time you're ready to cook! And don't deviate from your shopping list next time you're at the store. Having foods that you aren't prepared to use can cost you money, even if they were on sale.

Plan your work, and then work your plan. Knowing where you're headed from the start can save you all kinds of time! Be prepared! Keep it simple!

Simple Pleasures

* Read a motivational book for fresh ideas and a new perspective.
* Do one major home maintenance project every year.
* Fishing is both relaxing and fun! It's a great way to spend time with the man in your life or an adventuresome friend.

Wisdom for Living

I need Your wisdom today as I begin. My plans are made, but You determine the outcome. Lord, I submit to Your outcome today.

Thinking of Others

It's not easy to get outside of ourselves and think of the needs of others. Too often we hesitate, wondering if what we have in mind will really bless another person. Today, don't hesitate—act! Do the thing you have on your mind to do for someone in need. It could make all the difference!

One of the most-appreciated gifts I ever received came from one of my dear neighbors after the birth of my first child. One day she appeared at my door and handed me a freshly baked apple pie. But the bigger gift was attached to the dish—a coupon redeemable for eight hours of free babysitting! I was a new mother, but I already knew this was a godsend. It was so reassuring to me to know there was someone available close by to babysit.

Take a moment to think of your husband, son, daughter, or a nearby friend. What simple thing could you do today to bless and encourage them? I had a friend who brought me a jar of her homemade chicken soup stock when I was down with a cold. I've never forgotten her simple thoughtfulness. Think of someone else today.

Simple Pleasures

- Can chicken stock. Nothing is more comforting than a hot bowl of soup.
- Order Chinese food for a depressed friend and have it delivered.
- Set a festive table and invite a next-door neighbor for a simple meal.

Wisdom for Living

Thank You, Lord, for the blessing of my family and friends. Touch each life today. Draw them closer to You. This is my heart's prayer for those I love.

First Things First

> But seek ye first the kingdom of
> God, and his righteousness; and
> all these things shall be added unto
> you.
>
> MATTHEW 6:33 (KJV)

Recently, I saw a sign that read, "I had my home clean last week—I'm sorry you missed it!" Does that sound like something you'd like to hang on your front door?

It may come as a surprise to you, but most of us have *never* had our home in perfect order. Today, let's purpose to change that—one day at a time!

Start by setting your mind to view this challenge as an exciting adventure, rather than drudgery, or a thankless job that you're stuck with.

We're going to begin by agreeing to only do a little each day. Don't tackle the whole house. You'll never make it, and you'll be tired and discouraged to boot. Decide to: "Do the worst first!" Sound incredible? You'll be amazed at how good you feel and how motivated you are to start tomorrow. Once the worst is done, everything else is so much easier.

Make a new To Do list each morning and give each item a priority number—1, 2, 3, etc. Do all the "ones" first! You may not get to the "twos" today, but you'll be ready to tackle them tomorrow. First things first!

Simple Pleasures

* It's not what you have, it's what you do with what you have that counts.
* Lay a fire so it's ready whenever you are—morning, noon, or night.
* Nestle in tonight with a good book and put your cares aside.

Wisdom for Living

Where to start? Lord, I feel overwhelmed again.
Calm my spirit. Focus my mind. I am looking to You.

Just Start

> *Prepare provisions for yourselves, for within three days you are to cross this Jordan, to go in to possess the land which the Lord your God is giving you, to possess it.*
>
> JOSHUA 1:11 (NASB)

Oh, how we struggle sometimes with the fact that we can't seem to find the time to get it all done. Can I let you in on a little secret? You'll never get it all done!

I don't know at what point that finally sank into my thinking, but grasping the reality of that one simple truth has revolutionized my life. Since it's the truth, how can we start to enjoy our lives a little more and worry about things a little less? Let me share some household tips to help put some "ease" into your days.

Make sure everyone in your family contributes to running the household—even the youngest children. You don't have to do it all, and they need to help.

Important: eliminate some work entirely. Now there's a thought. Who says you have to iron everything?

Use small amounts of time to your best advantage. It's amazing what can be done in five- or ten-minute blocks of time. And leave yourself some open-ended time for a spur-of-the-moment activity. Don't cram your appointment book full.

The key is to start now! Don't wait to find more time. Along the way—enjoy!

Simple Pleasures

Afternoon tea...the mere chink of cups and saucers
tunes the mind to happy repose.

—GEORGE GISSING

Wisdom for Living

Lord, You instructed Your people to prepare for what was to come. Grant me Your wisdom and grace to hear Your voice and to consider my ways before You.

The Daily Need for Strength

Watch therefore, for ye know neither the day nor the hour wherein the Son of man cometh.

MATTHEW 25:13 (KJV)

I've learned that the most amazing infusions of God's strength happen when I'm taking the risk of obeying God. I'm astonished at how my Lord can take a tiny step of faith—and turn it into a strong leap for His kingdom.

You may be a young mom with children at home, or a dad whose teenagers are in trouble. You may be struggling with illness or working at a job that saps your spirit. Whatever set of circumstances you face today, purpose in your heart to hear the voice of God and obey whatever you believe He is leading you to do.

We need to exercise our faith by turning to our God when life seems too much—or maybe even just too *daily!* The Bible tells us the truth about this: We are weak, but He is strong!

His mighty arms are outstretched to you today. He is ready to pour out His strength upon you. He understands your need and is ready to supply. All you have to do is to take hold! Take hold of Him. Your example as you turn to the Lord in your pain and weakness will encourage others to do the same.

Simple Pleasures

- Indulge yourself in a therapeutic massage or makeover.
- Call one of your favorite people and plan to linger over a meal.
- Meditate on the abundance of your blessings.

Wisdom for Living

In this one area, Lord, I can't seem to find Your way or hear Your voice. But today, I will turn—even if it is in the smallest way—just a little more toward You.

"Fix Me, Lord"

> Heal the sick, raise the dead, cleanse the lepers, cast out demons; freely you received, freely give.
>
> MATTHEW 10:8 (NASB)

What a sense of satisfaction to fix a child's broken toy, or "make it all better" with a Band-Aid or a kiss. I also enjoy immensely the process of restoring old, beat-up furniture. With a little paint, a yard or two of fabric, and some imagination, almost any worn-out item can be restored to beauty or usefulness.

I find such joy in my own small efforts at restoration. Over the years, I've found it's also a wonderful way to find some moments of fellowship with a daughter or a friend. Plan to do a restoration project together. Find an old piece of furniture, a garden bench, or an antique chair and go to work. Before you know it, you've not only salvaged something of worth, but you've created a few great memories beside.

I've often wondered if my heavenly Father finds the same kind of joy in restoring me. For restoration is exactly what He promises us through Scripture. "He restores my soul," sings the psalmist. Fixed, redeemed, and shining good as new. It isn't always an easy process, removing years of grime and dirt. But the handiwork of the Father is always magnificent—magnificently "all better!"

Simple Pleasures

Be Thou our great Deliverer still, Thou Lord of life
and death; Restore and quicken, soothe and
bless with Thine almighty breath. To hands that work and
eyes that see, give wisdom's heavenly lore, That whole and sick, and
weak and strong, may praise Thee evermore.

—EDWARD PLUMPTRE

Wisdom for Living

*God, I feel so broken. Take my wounded parts and make me whole.
I look to You, my Great Physician.*

The Habit of Habit

> Go to the ant, you sluggard;
> consider its ways and be wise!
>
> PROVERBS 6:6

One of the most important skills you can ever learn in this life is how to form habits—how to get into the habit of habits.

Why habits? It's one more way to organize our time and our lives. And it's one more step toward giving priority to what God has called us to do with our lives! It starts with handling the routine jobs in our lives. This is where "habit" comes in.

Start by thinking before you do routine jobs. The way that you perform basic tasks is usually the result of habit, not logic. Is there a better way? Why does a half-hour job often take twice as long as planned? It's probably because you estimated only the working time—perhaps you forgot the time it takes to get everything set up! Make it a habit to think before you start.

Also, make it a habit to return everything to its proper place. Nothing wastes time like not knowing where you put something you need now!

Now reward yourself for doing such a great job. Put your feet up, and enjoy a cup of tea and a good book.

Simple Pleasures

We read books to find out who we are...[it] is an essential guide to our understanding of what we ourselves are and may become.

—URSULA K. LEGUIN

Wisdom for Living

Bolster my spirit, Lord, as I bolster my will. As I choose to follow You, enlarge my heart to hear Your voice.

Get Comfortable with Never Being Finished

Being confident of this, that he who began a good work in you will carry it on to completion until the day of Christ Jesus.

PHILIPPIANS 1:6

Have you ever wished you could just be finished with all those tasks and chores you have in mind to accomplish around your home? I want to let you in on a little secret. If your goal is to create a welcoming haven that offers peace and beauty to all who enter in, your work will never be finished. It's going to be a process. So let's talk about how to make this really work!

First, don't be afraid to change your home as your needs and priorities change. Get rid of items that don't work for you or your family any longer. Always be on the search for ideas that will make your living space more comfortable and relaxing. A home is a dynamic place, just like the people who live there, so change should be expected and planned for.

Now, I don't mean living in the chaos of constant construction, or waiting a year to put up pictures in a new apartment. But don't feel like it has to be all perfect—or even finished. And don't be afraid to change it back if you don't like it.

By all means, keep dreaming! And enjoy the process of watching dreams come true!

Simple Pleasures
- Make yourself a pitcher of ice water and drink it through the day.
- Take a few moments before entertaining to compose yourself.
- Host an author or artist in your home to share their work with friends.

Wisdom for Living
Father, I know my life won't be finished until the day I stand before You. So I ask that You would make me content to enjoy my lifelong journey to You, instead of always thinking about getting one more thing done.

46

Little by Little

Little by little I will drive them out before you, until you have increased enough to take possession of the land.

EXODUS 23:30

"Little by little" is a biblical principle, but it's so hard for us to make it work. Why is that? Why can't we seem to find our way to "little by little"? I guess it's our human nature that wants to go from "big to bigger." Let's take housecleaning, for example—just saying the words makes me tired!

We all want more hours in our day, don't we? Let me share a couple of hints to make those cleaning jobs go as quickly as possible.

First of all, change those big tasks into smaller tasks. If cleaning the refrigerator seems totally overwhelming, do the bottom shelf on Monday, the middle shelf on Tuesday, the fruit and vegetable drawers on Wednesday, and the outside on Thursday. You've got the idea! Big projects become more manageable when you break them into smaller parts.

Here's the best part! Treat yourself for a job well done. You've earned it! Enjoy a cup of tea, and take some of that time you've saved for a quiet time with God. It will restore your soul.

Simple Pleasures

- Let "make life cozy" be your motto.
- Read a book about an artist. Glimpse the creative spirit.
- Take a class along your lines of interest at a local community college.

Wisdom for Living

*I need patience, Lord. There is so much before me, and
I cannot carry these responsibilities without Your strength and wisdom.
I ask that You restore my soul this day.*

More Hours in Your Day

> And God called the firmament Heaven. And the evening and the morning were the second day.
>
> GENESIS 1:8 (KJV)

Do you want to know how to get more hours in your day? I certainly do. In fact, I've spent much of my life working toward that goal and helping other men and women do the same.

Well, here's one of my secrets: start your day the night before! That's simple enough, isn't it? And it's actually biblical, too. The Bible suggests that each new day starts in the evening and goes through the following daytime. So let's see how that can work in our thinking.

Set the breakfast table the night before. Gather the wash and sort it. Set up the coffeepot for morning and make a list of what must be done the next day.

When morning finally rolls around, the day is already well underway for you. Get up early! Put in the first load of wash, shower, and dress.

Then before anyone is up, grab a cup of coffee or tea and spend a few moments thanking God for another day, for good health, and for filling your life with meaning and purpose.

Today, try beginning your tomorrow tonight. See what God will do!

Simple Pleasures

To be happy at home is the ultimate result of all ambition,
the end to which every enterprise and labor tends...

—SAMUEL JOHNSON

Wisdom for Living

You are the God of every moment. Teach me to
order my ways even as You direct my paths, Lord.
Thank You for Your instructive presence in my life.

March

MARTHA, MARTHA

More of Everything, Please

You were faithful with a few things, I will put you in charge of many things; enter into the joy of your master.

MATTHEW 25:23 (NASB)

"More storage, more time, more money!" It's the cry of most every frustrated homemaker! There just never seem to be enough cabinets, cupboards, or shelves, enough time to get all our projects done, or enough money to do all we want to do.

But stop! Is it really more that we need, or less? Try rearranging your existing space. Look for wasted "air space" and organize more efficiently. Things you use often should be in easy-to-access places. Save your difficult-to-reach places for what you seldom need.

Give one item away every day. It's tough, but it will give you more room and cut down on the "stuff" you have to manage.

Today, determine to think outside the box. Assume that you have plenty of everything, and think about how you can make your life less cluttered, less time-consuming, less costly. The idea is to organize your life so that you have time for the important things. Remember that by using small amounts of time and resources faithfully, you can accomplish great things!

Simple Pleasures

It is the first mild day of March;
Each minute sweeter than before...
There is a blessing in the air...

—WILLIAM WORDSWORTH

Wisdom for Living

Heavenly Father, You are the Creator. Teach me to be creative just as You are. Help me to express Your love and likeness in all I do today.

All These Things

But my God shall supply all your need according to his riches in glory by Christ Jesus.

PHILIPPIANS 4:19 (KJV)

Unless you have unlimited resources, you can't have everything. Here are a few tips to help you maximize what you do have. Remember, the key is simplicity.

If you want to save money and time on redecorating, try adding small, round end tables with table skirts and overdrapes to your living room. They're much less expensive than most end tables, and the fabric will add color and interest to your room.

Buy in bulk when items are on sale. I receive so many catalogs that I now shop by phone. It's amazing how much time and money I save.

Smart shoppers take advantage of clearance sales after Christmas, Easter, and the Fourth of July. You'll find bargains galore during end-of-season sales. Make a day of it with friends!

Above all, keep God's comforting promise in mind as you trust Him for your needs: "Seek first His kingdom and His righteousness, and all these things will be added to you" (Matthew 6:33 NASB).

Simple Pleasures

- Hang out in the stacks at your local bookstore for a cozy evening.
- Buy a porch swing or hammock—and then use it.
- Be on the lookout for the first signs of spring.

Wisdom for Living

Lord, You are my desire. All I have belongs to You. Teach me to use my resources wisely. Multiply my efforts for Your eternal glory.

A Memorable Meal

The eyes of all wait upon thee; and thou givest them their meat in due season.

PSALM 145:15 (KJV)

Oh, how I long sometimes for the good old days, when our family gathered every night around the dinner table and shared events of the day. Life seemed a little less busy then and there weren't so many options to keep us away from the ritual of evening meals. It's sad to see family meals becoming a thing of the past for so many.

Tonight, buck the trend. Plan a memorable mealtime with family and friends. What makes a mealtime memorable? The attractive way you set the table says, "I care enough to do a little extra." A simple centerpiece can establish a mood, especially if it includes candles, creating a spirit of warmth at mealtime. Obviously, food takes the starring role, so healthy, tasty fare is best!

Think of Jesus—even He chose to share a special meal with His 12 disciples during His final hours. The fellowship with these dearest of earthly companions must have given Him great comfort as He prepared for the trials ahead.

Make the most of these times—they are times to cherish! And they nurture more than the body; they feed the soul and prepare us for living full, productive lives.

Simple Pleasures

Cooking is a bit like painting; strong herbs are reminiscent of oils; delicate ones, of watercolors.

—MICHAEL GUERARD

Wisdom for Living

You have satisfied my soul, Jesus. You are the One I turn to to find life, and joy, and peace, and pardon. All my springs are in You.

The Openness of God's Life

She openeth her mouth with wisdom; and in her tongue is the law of kindness.

PROVERBS 31:26 (KJV)

Sometimes we think that for something to be truly meaningful it must look and feel religious or "spiritual." How far from the truth that is! Often, those things that touch another person in a deeply spiritual way are simple acts of kindness and goodness that demonstrate the love of God. Consider the following ideas:

Frame a print or lovely thought and deliver it to a discouraged friend.

Call someone unexpectedly just to say, "It's been a while since we talked. I wondered how you were."

Jot down the words from an old Christian hymn and send it in a card to an older person you know. What a blessing those old hymns of the faith can be!

Find an old snapshot of a great time with a family member or friend and drop it in the mail with a note, "Haven't we had some special times?"

Keep your life simple and open before God! Let His creative spirit motivate your acts of kindness and generosity. You never know what simple gesture might encourage someone who is struggling to understand the love of God.

Simple Pleasures

* Weed your garden and feel the pulsing of reawakened life.
* Gather a few children and find a high spot to watch the sunset.
* Lie on the floor and put on your stereo headphones and favorite music.

Wisdom for Living

You, Lord, can take the most simple things and touch them with eternity. Guide and direct me today so that my simple life will count for Your Kingdom.

Can We Make the Kitchen a Spiritual Place?

He hath made every thing beautiful in his time…

Can we make the kitchen a spiritual place? I might be walking on theological eggshells, but I think the answer is yes! There's something about that room of the house that reveals—and sets—the tenor for the entire household.

Keeping kitchen clutter under control is the first step. It can be a frustrating task—but it's not impossible. Starting with the cupboards closest to the sink, pull everything out. Wipe out the shelves and refresh them with contact paper. For all the things you're not using—either put them in a "throw away" bag, a "give away" bag, or a box marked, "kitchen overflow." Put the things you don't use very often on the highest shelves. Items you use daily go back into the cupboards in easily accessible places.

What about gadgets and utensils? Put them in a crock and tie a bow around it. It looks cute and keeps your counters uncluttered.

What's so spiritual about all this? The next time your husband or children need a hug or a listening ear, you'll be ready, with the heart of the home under control.

Simple Pleasures

* Create an herbal nosegay to scent your towels.
* Crawl into a warm robe for that first cup of coffee.
* Place a few roses in small bottles beside your bed.

Wisdom for Living

I sometimes feel as if I just don't have enough for everyone in my life. Fill me with Your grace, dear Lord, so that I have all that I need to touch the lives of others. I need You, Jesus.

Don't Answer the Phone!

His lord said unto him, "Well done, thou good and faithful servant."

MATTHEW 25:21 (KJV)

It couldn't be simpler—just don't answer the phone! "But how can I just let it ring?" Here's how—just let it ring. Or purchase an answering machine and let the "mechanical secretary" protect your time until you're ready to make your calls.

There are only a few things in life that we can truly control, but we can control the phone. In our day, we've become slaves to the telephone—in our homes, our cars, and everywhere we go. The ringing phone triggers a knee-jerk reaction that compels us to answer. Unfortunately, for just that moment, it also robs us of focus and, in a small way, disturbs our peace and tranquillity.

How often does the phone ring just as you're sitting down to dinner? Don't answer the phone at mealtimes. Let your family know that they are much more important than the unknown caller.

Certainly, there are times when we need to answer the phone—but you decide when. Don't let others control your life and alter your activities. You have the power to decide. It's as simple as that!

Simple Pleasures

People who live in cities need tranquillity most.

—CHRISTINE GUERARD

Wisdom for Living

Lord, I need to make solitude a priority in my life. Help me find that place of quiet and meditation before You. Only You can transform my life.

Imitating Christ's Humility

Therefore I take pleasure in infirmities, in reproaches, in necessities, in persecutions, in distresses for Christ's sake: for when I am weak, then am I strong.

2 CORINTHIANS 12:10 (KJV)

In a world bombarded with self-esteem issues, it's easy to become confused about what it means to be humble. How do we experience healthy self-esteem as well as real humility? Since the Bible clearly tells us that we're to do nothing out of selfish ambition—that in humility, we're to consider others better than ourselves—these are issues that we had better sort out.

First, evaluate your abilities. Actually write them down in a journal. Under each, write at least ten strengths and weaknesses. What are you going to do with your strengths? What plan do you have for turning your weaknesses into strengths?

Next, list three areas where you are willing to serve. Volunteer your services in one of these areas this week. What does service have to do with humility? Well, humility has three elements that are brought out and strengthened when we really give ourselves to serve others: First, true humility recognizes your need for God. Second, true humility realistically evaluates your capacities. Third, a truly humble person is always willing to serve. This is the recipe for humility and health.

Simple Pleasures

* Place a pretty glass and a bottle of mineral water in your guest room.
* Donate your old magazines or books to the annual library fundraiser.
* A hot fudge sundae with bananas and nuts is a special treat.

Wisdom for Living

What could I do today, Lord, to be a blessing to someone else?
My flesh cries out for attention, but I know I have everything I need.
Show me how to be a blessing to someone today.

Where's the Welcome?

Accept one another, then, just as Christ accepted you, in order to bring praise to God.

ROMANS 15:7

When decorating your home, where do you want to focus? What do you want people to see first when they enter the room? A room's focal point is its center of gravity, so you'll want to arrange the room to play up that focus.

Also, consider a room's "body language"—lighting, comfort, visual balance, and utility. One interesting thing to remember: a room can actually appear to "open its arms" to people, or to "turn its back" on them. Even chairs grouped around a fireplace can be angled so they appear to invite visitors over. Make your home inviting—give it the feel of love and welcome!

In Matthew 11:28 (NASB), Jesus says: "Come to Me, all who are weary and heavy-laden, and I will give you rest!" The same spirit of welcome that He extends to us can be expressed to others in our homes and our lives.

Maybe you need to do a little rearranging today to make your rooms more inviting. Maybe you need to do a little rearranging of your time to make room for someone who needs a gentle touch.

Simple Pleasures

* Work on a jigsaw puzzle—it develops patience and is relaxing, too.
* Visit the nearest university library and study a topic you're interested in.
* Go for a walk. Take in the scenery and breathe the fresh air.

Wisdom for Living

How can I accept others, Lord? I can't even accept myself. Thank You for accepting me just as I am. Today, help me to come to You completely.

Organizing Your Kids

All your sons will be taught by the Lord, and great will be your children's peace.

ISAIAH 54:13

If you have children, you've got to keep it simple! Here are some tips that have worked for me. And if you don't have children, these tips can work in some way for you as well.

Have one area where the children place all their school items. I used colored bins by the front door where each one would put his or her gym clothes, homework, and schoolbooks. This saved a lot of last-minute hunting for items before dashing out the door. Color-code your children. Jenny knew that the yellow towels were hers, and Brad knew that his were blue. Make sure each child has a place to hang clothes and store belongings.

Put the artwork of your young Van Gogh in his or her own folder. Some of the extra artwork can be used in wrapping grandparents' gifts.

Order is a part of the universe, and the more we order our steps, the more we participate in the order of God's world. What is it the Bible says? "Train up a child in the way that he should go." Teach your children how to order their belongings. It's a gift that will last for a lifetime.

Simple Pleasures

* Read the *Madeline* books to your child and pretend you're in France.
* Check out music from the library and learn about classical composers.
* Whip up a batch of scones and serve hot with butter, jam, and a pot of tea.

Wisdom for Living

I need to teach those around me, but Lord, I still need to be taught. I come to You today and ask for a teachable heart! Please, Lord, teach me!

Simplicity— Even in Meal Planning

Consider the lilies of the field, how they grow; they toil not, neither do they spin: And yet I say unto you, that even Solomon in all his glory was not arrayed like one of these.

MATTHEW 6:28-29 (KJV)

Seven hundred fifty meals a year! That's the quota for the average homemaker. Meals are a major part of our lives. It behooves us to keep them simple!

Years ago, I found myself serving as a short-order cook at breakfast. Everyone had their own likes and dislikes, and I was trying to please them all. Something needed to change!

My plan evolved over time, but in the end, I decided to sit down once a week and plan each day's breakfast in advance. As I determined the menu and wrote my shopping list, I incorporated each family member's favorite breakfast one morning each week. On Monday, it might be Brad's favorite—French toast. On Tuesday, it could be fried eggs—over medium—for my husband, Bob. You get the idea. Sunday was "cook's choice," or Bob cooked that morning, which was always a treat for me!

It became such a pleasure to cook breakfast with this system that I very quickly expanded my planning to include all of our meals. It saved time and money, and it became a privilege to plan lovingly for my family.

Simple Pleasures

- Make fresh-squeezed orange juice a part of your morning ritual.
- Cultivate a sense of paradise by bringing greenery inside.
- Pack a light lunch and take off. Who knows where you will end up?

Wisdom for Living

Your provision for me is unspeakable, Lord. Day in and day out You provide for all my needs. Let me rejoice in You—the God of my life.

Make Life Cozy

And the rain descended, and the floods came, and the winds blew, and beat upon that house; and it fell not: for it was founded upon a rock.

MATTHEW 7:25 (KJV)

I love Saturdays. In our family, Saturday was always yardwork day! With everyone pitching in, it wasn't long before we were all enjoying the smell of fresh-cut grass and that amazing sound of the sprinkler on the lawn. Summer is in full swing!

Or how about this one? The days are getting shorter, and there's a late afternoon nip in the air. Before you know it, it's time to build that first autumn fire in the fireplace and settle in with a good book or movie. Fall has arrived!

The things that hold the richest associations for us are often simple sights, sounds, or smells: chocolate chip cookies baking in the oven, a scented candle burning on a dresser, soft pillows fluffed up on the sofa. These are inexpensive ways of making a house feel like home. Even a half-worked puzzle or a needlework project in a basket can give your house that "at home" feel. Regardless of the season, there are always little ways to make *your* home cozy and inviting!

Proverbs says: "By wisdom a house is built...through knowledge its rooms are filled with rare and beautiful treasures!" Make life cozy today!

Simple Pleasures

- Buy a piece of lace and drape it over a shelf or small table.
- Everyone needs a gardening hat to call their own.
- Rest a small painting or card on an easel and place it on a tabletop.

Wisdom for Living

I love to come before You, Lord Jesus, to rest in Your presence and to delight in who You are. Nothing satisfies my heart like You do.

The Spirit of Welcome

You are the light of the world...

MATTHEW 5:14

Your home is a reflection of everyone who lives there. It may be hard to believe, but it is possible for your music stand and your son's baseball trophy to peacefully coexist in the same living space! Your home can reflect an attitude that says, "People are accepted here for who they are." In addition, of course, the welcome comes from *you*.

The spirit of welcome begins in your own heart, in your own attitudes. It has its birth in your willingness to accept yourself as God's child and to be grateful for your place in God's family. It carries over into how you view others.

With the spirit of welcome in your heart, you can begin to see your encounters with people each day as gifts, instead of viewing them as hindrances and distractions. Close relationships become one of God's true treasures in our lives.

People of all mixes and measures are gifts from God. That is the basis of an attitude that makes a smile and a hug as important to your spirit of welcome as a candle and pot of stew!

Simple Pleasures

I had three chairs in my house: one for solitude,
two for friendship, three for society.

—HENRY DAVID THOREAU

Wisdom for Living

My light feels a bit dim today, but I come to You, the light of the world. Light the fire of Your life within me once again, that I might shine for You.

Surprise Impressions

A happy heart makes the face cheerful, but heartache crushes the spirit.

The best kind of first impression is a personal one! One of the most charming and surprising first impressions I ever experienced was at the home of a dear friend.

I was on my way to visit her at her home in Scottsdale, Arizona. She picked me up at the airport, and we had a lovely visit on the way out to her home. Winding through the desert, I already felt at home and welcome. When we finally arrived and pulled up to her garage, the automatic door opener whirred and we drove inside. There on the wall of the garage was a big blackboard with the words, "Welcome Emmy." I was so pleased and surprised. What a warm and creative greeting!

My friend had thought ahead about how I would be entering her home—then she thoughtfully positioned her greeting. Her kind, simple gesture made me relax all the more as we settled in for a wonderful visit.

When your guests approach your drive or your walk or your steps, greet them with something that is cheerful and personal.

Simple Pleasures

It's nice to return home each day to something intensely personal.

—STANLEY BARROWS

Wisdom for Living

Lord, I want the welcome mat of my life to say, "I care about you" to those around me. Show me what that will mean this day as I seek to serve You.

Set the Record Straight

Every good gift and every p[...]
gift is from above, and cometh
down from the Father of lights,
with whom is no variableness,
neither shadow of turning.

JAMES 1:17 (KJV)

It isn't easy to keep our lives organized and on track. It isn't easy to keep our minds and hearts that way either. Here are few ideas to help you with both.

I've kept a mini-notebook for several years called The Lord Provides. I've listed each gift that I've received and from whom. It's beautiful to see how the Lord leads others to meet our needs and desires. This wonderful notebook has also helped me to tell someone at a later date how much their gift meant to me.

Whenever I receive an invitation, I've found that if I simply attach the invitation to my kitchen calendar in the month the event will take place, I won't have to search for it weeks later. The time, the place, and especially the spelling of people's names are right where I know I can find them.

And don't forget to spend a few moments every day keeping your personal desk space and calendar organized. It's a great habit to get into.

Now that you've saved so much time, treat yourself to a lovely cup of tea and some quiet time with the Lord.

Simple Pleasures

The manner of giving is worth more than the gift.

—PIERRE CORNEILLE

Wisdom for Living

Lord, I could never begin to record all Your benefits to me.
They are as unfathomable as the stars in the sky.
How majestic is Your name in all the earth.

*e Gift of
ininity*

*And the king loved Esther above
all the women, and she obtained
grace and favour in his sight more
than all the virgins.*

ESTHER 2:17 (KJV)

I encourage you to pass along your God-given feminine spirit to your daughters. We do it when we teach girls the secrets of caring for themselves and for others.

We do it when we share our pride and skills in such classic domestic arts as cooking, sewing, and knitting.

Try taking an afternoon off to play "dress up" with a little girl in your life. Deck yourselves out in your finery, and visit a local tea room for ice cream or a muffin. Or in the spring, take a child for a "senses walk." Smell the roses—see how many different fragrances you can detect. Close your eyes and listen for different sounds. These kinds of activities allow the feminine spirit of a girl to be nurtured and developed.

More importantly, don't miss any opportunity to teach biblical values—caring for ourselves and others. Talk about the joy of creating and shaping a godly home. It is one of our priorities, but it can also be such fun!

It's so simple to value the gifts of God, and femininity is one of them!

Simple Pleasures

- Enhance your hygiene with a new bath salt or fragrant body lotion.
- Try the free samples of perfume given away in stores. Buy one you like.
- Save old perfume bottles—they make ideal bud vases.

Wisdom for Living

*Thank You, Father, that I am Your daughter. I belong to You,
and therefore, I am at rest in Your grace and favor.*

The Strength of a Woman

"If it pleases the king," she said, "and if he regards me with favor and thinks it the right thing to do, and if he is pleased with me, let an order be written..."

ESTHER 8:5

Many of us are confused about what true femininity really is. No doubt, God created the woman to be tender and full of gentleness. But we are sadly mistaken if we take that quality of femininity to mean something weak. Nothing could be farther from the truth! It takes physical stamina, emotional strength, and spiritual courage to be a woman. And that's not a modern feminist philosophy. Consider Esther.

Queen Esther risked her life to save her people. But she understood God's call and responded. What a strong, resolute woman! She defied an adversary. She was full of the strength of God and accomplished what He had called her to do.

Or what about Sarah Edwards, wife of the famous theologian, Jonathan Edwards? With no modern conveniences, she ran a household and raised 11 children. She taught her children to work hard and to respect others. She surrounded all her teaching with her love for God and for each child.

Even my own sweet mother, who ran a little dress shop to support us after my father died, was a woman of true strength. It was she who taught me to love beauty and reach out in love to others.

Simple Pleasures

Beauty, old yet ever new; eternal voice and inward word.

—JOHN GREENLEAF WHITTIER

Wisdom for Living

*Dear Lord, help me to not confuse weakness and tenderness,
or a hardened heart and true strength. Help me to understand
what it means to stand for You and yet serve You with humility.
Only You can grant such wisdom. Thank You, Lord.*

The Art of Focus

> And thine ears shall hear a word
> behind thee, saying, This is the
> way, walk ye in it.
>
> Isaiah 30:21 (KJV)

The key to finishing those many tasks around your home is *focus*.

Choose a regular time every day to organize your work. Some women find that a few minutes in the early morning, before the day is underway, are the best. Others like the comfort of doing this in the evening so that they awake with a plan already in place. Whatever you decide, stick with it. It will soon become a habit.

Use a single notebook for your To Do list and the notes that go along with those projects. Make this your power center and focus on those areas that you've established as priorities.

Next, develop the ability to focus on the part and not the whole. It will take practice, but it can be done. Here's how. Divide difficult problems into instant tasks. In other words, clean one shelf or drawer at a time. If the whole is too large to do in a day, take two or three days.

Now, reward yourself for all your efforts and "unfocus" for a few minutes with a good book, a cup of tea, or second cup of coffee.

Simple Pleasures

Gazing on beautiful things acts on my soul,
which thirsts for heavenly light.

—Michelangelo

Wisdom for Living

I want to hear Your voice above all others. It thrills me so! I long to live—and someday die—in Your arms, dear Jesus. I set my heart on You today.

An Effective Prayer Life

When you pray, go into your room, close the door and pray to your Father, who is unseen.

MATTHEW 6:6

Many years ago, I developed a Prayer Planner to help me pray more effectively for others. Today, I still find it to be one of the most important tools I have ever developed for organizing the most important area of my life. Here's how I did it.

I took an 6" x 9" loose-leaf notebook and divided it into seven sections—one for each day of the week. That makes it easy for me to remember to pray for certain people and projects. Monday is for my family, Tuesday is for my church, and so on.

Next, I made room on each page for photos of the people I'm praying for, along with their interests, their needs, and special things to remember about them. This is a wonderful way to personalize my prayers and remind me of each person's uniqueness.

As I begin my quiet time, I generally start by reading a brief devotional message or prayer. After spending time in my Bible, I'm ready to turn to my planner for that day's prayer list. What a tremendous feeling to know that I can cover each person in prayer, and that no one has been left out. It's been great for me. Why not try it?

Simple Pleasures

- Pray for our country and our leaders.
- Pray for your pastor and the ministry of your church.
- Pray for yourself, that you might find the path to simplicity.

Wisdom for Living

Thank You that Your Spirit knows how to pray for us, even when we do not. I rely on Your Holy Spirit to make the depths of my heart known to You this day.

The Beauty of a Junk Drawer

Wherefore, if God so clothe the grass of the field...shall he not much more clothe you, O ye of little faith?

Matthew 6:30 (KJV)

We all have a junk drawer! There just doesn't seem to be any way to eliminate it. But we *can* take the junk and clean it up. Have you ever seen a really organized junk drawer? It's actually a beautiful thing! Here are some ways to get yours in order.

One of the things that works best for me is a plastic silverware tray. It's where Bob and I keep the hammer, screwdriver, and other tools. I even add a couple of small artichoke jars to store hooks, nails, and thumbtacks—all those little things we didn't know what to do with.

Another idea someone gave me was to use an egg carton. Cut apart the cartons so you have small sections. Then the screws, picture hangers, and extra key rings fit in your nicely organized junk drawer!

Batteries can also be stored in the junk drawer, but find a small box so they don't roll around and contribute to confusion. The same is true for pens and pencils.

The whole idea is to keep it simple!

Simple Pleasures

* Go fly a kite!
* Make a sand castle on the beach.
* Give your brain a nap—daydream.

Wisdom for Living

Help me, Lord, to bring order where there is disorder.
Help me to begin today.

The Proper Adornment

Your beauty should not come from outward adornment, such as braided hair and the wearing of gold jewelry and fine clothes.

1 PETER 3:3

Nothing is more fun and satisfying than decorating your home—making it *you!* Each of us wants our home to be a thing of beauty, however we may define that beauty, and even though we may be on a tight budget. We want our home to be comfortable and cozy for ourselves and our family.

I've discovered that what really matters most is creating an atmosphere of sharing. The most wonderful adornment to your home is your spirit of hospitality, your willingness to open your home and your life with others.

You don't need to wait until everything's perfect. It will never be! After all, people live in your house! Something will always need painting or replacing. It just won't ever be perfect—no matter how hard you try!

Love what you have and invite others in to share the bounty. Your gracious welcome will fill the gaps and make the problems seem to disappear.

When you have second thoughts about sharing because everything isn't just how you want it, put on the proper adornment—a thankful heart—and share anyway.

Simple Pleasures

A little thing comforts us because a little thing afflicts us.

—BLAISE PASCAL

Wisdom for Living

I lift my heart to You today, Father in Heaven, and ask that You would give me the gift of gratitude. Let me exhibit a grateful heart in all I say and do.

Work the System

In his heart a man plans his course, but the Lord determines his steps.

PROVERBS 16:9

Oh, if only life were simpler! Isn't this the heart's cry for many of us? Through the years, I've shared with women how important I believe organization is to our peace of mind. Without it, we can never quite find the time we need to do the truly important things.

More Hours In My Day was founded as a ministry to help encourage and teach women how to maximize the minutes and hours of each day, with one purpose in mind—to give them more time with God, family, friends, and community!

Bob and I pray continually that men and women who use our materials will be impacted not only in their homes and lives, but in their spirits as well. Not surprisingly, there seems to be a connection between the two!

Take a moment today to think back on some of the principles for organization we've shared and see if it's time to renew your commitment to put one or more of them into practice today. It's not only having a system that works; you've also got to work the system! God bless you today!

Simple Pleasures

- A piece of copper is a beautiful decoration, and it's functional, too.
- Place fresh flowers in a pail of water or the sink until you're ready to place them around the house.
- Serve a tiny hot towel to your guests before dinner begins.

Wisdom for Living

Back to basics, Lord. I need Your help today to implement some things I know I must do to make my life look more like Yours. It's by Your grace, Lord; only by Your grace.

April

THE BEAUTY OF THE ORDINARY

The Meaning of Home

Lord, thou hast been our dwelling place in all generations.

PSALM 90:1 (KJV)

We all need a place where we can unwind and regroup, where we can get in touch with who we are and what God has planned for us. In our busy lives, home is just as important as it always has been, and maybe more so.

Home is as much a state of the heart and spirit as it is a specific place. It doesn't take a lot of money or even a lot of time to make a welcoming refuge. What it does require is a determination to think beyond necessities and go for what enriches the soul.

A home is where real life happens. But it doesn't happen all at once! It's a lifelong, step-by-step process of discovery. It's taken me more than 30 years to develop the systems that help me maintain order—and I'm still learning. Many things that are truly important in life take a little extra time. Let God use you to bring a sense of comfort and welcome to a troubled world. Important, indeed!

There are lots of voices trying to tell us how to achieve the happy, healthy lifestyle we all desire. But remember, it starts with *home*.

Simple Pleasures

There are few hours in life more agreeable than the hour dedicated to the ceremony known as tea.

—HENRY JAMES

Wisdom for Living

Thank You for the gift of my home, Lord. I pray today that Your presence in my home and in my life will be apparent to each person who comes within these walls.

From Ordinary to Special

But we have this treasure in earthen vessels, that the excellency of the power may be of God, and not of us.

2 CORINTHIANS 4:7 (KJV)

The next time you decide to throw something away, stop and think for a moment about other possible uses you might find for that broken or worn out object. Discover the joy of taking something ordinary and making it into something special! Simple ideas can really make your home sparkle!

For instance, that cracked mug or old teapot with a broken lid can show off a lovely flower arrangement. An old wall-hanging can be reused in the garage to give that ordinarily uninteresting space some visual appeal.

For an extra-homey dinner, try using a quilt that rarely comes out of the closet as a tablecloth. Or drape a worn-out sofa with a bright quilt to camouflage and decorate at the same time. Collect odd-shaped perfume bottles and display them on a mirrored tray. Or use tiny, cute jam jars to organize your nails, bolts, and screws.

Isn't this just what God is doing with us? Doesn't He take what is broken and worn out in our lives and remake it into something special? Our lives can radiate His love and demonstrate His care.

Simple Pleasures

- Walk or run in an early spring rain.
- Try your hand at writing a poem as an expression of your hope in God.
- Set aside a day for doing nothing. Curl up in bed with a good book.

Wisdom for Living

Your power, Lord. Your glory. Today, take this earthen vessel and pour Your abundant life through me into the lives of those I love.

73

Rethinking a Room, and Our Lives

> Do not conform any longer to the pattern of this world, but be transformed by the renewing of your mind.
>
> ROMANS 12:2

There you are, standing in the middle of your living room, wondering what to do to make it look fabulous. Where do you start? Whether you're staring at four empty walls or a roomful of furniture, you start at the same place—with the big picture!

Starting with the big picture means evaluating the basic furnishings that you have or that you may still need. Once you have the big pieces arranged in the room, you can add or subtract other elements to complete the picture.

Our walk with the Lord requires much the same process. When was the last time you stood in the middle of your life, wondering what the Lord was up to and how you could cooperate with some of the rearranging He might be trying to do? Maybe He's meddling with your thought life or your attitudes. Maybe He's trying to get your attention regarding some of your personal habits. Maybe it's just time for some changes in your perspectives or in a relationship here or there.

Whatever it is, John 1:3-4 (NASB) tells us, "All things came into being through Him...in Him was life, and the life was the Light of men." Get the big picture?

Simple Pleasures

* Save your old rose petals and show them off in a pretty basket.
* Attend a classical concert and let your mind float away on the beauty.
* Reorganize the freezer section of your refrigerator.

Wisdom for Living

I know it is so easy to lose my perspective, Lord, and to get caught up in things that don't really matter. Establish an eternal perspective in my heart, and make that the reason for all I do.

Treasure Hunting

Let your conversation be without covetousness; and be content with such things as ye have.

HEBREWS 13:5 (KJV)

It's so tempting to run out and buy the newest thing, the one that we just have to have. But how about trying something else new? Let's discover a new use for something old.

The best decorating bargains are ones that cost us little, and that recycle someone else's used materials. Family and friends can be great resources. Garage sales, swap meets, and estate sales are also dependable sources of decorating bargains. It shouldn't take more than a few weekends of treasure hunting to locate the best sources for your use. That old saying, "Something old, something new, something borrowed..." doesn't have to be just a wedding formula—it can also be the secret to decorating beautifully on a budget.

And while you're hunting, here's something else to think about from 2 Corinthians 5:17: "If any [woman] is in Christ, [she] is a new creature; old things have passed away; behold, all things have become new." God doesn't just throw us away, He intends for us to become new creatures in Him! What a wonderful promise of hope.

Simple Pleasures

* Feel the warmth of the sun on your bare skin.
* Savor the smell of bacon sizzling on the stove, first thing in the morning.
* Smile at finding money tucked away in the cushions of the couch.

Wisdom for Living

Lord, satisfy my soul with Your joy, love, and forgiveness, and I will be satisfied. Everything else is just window dressing.

Pillowcases

*See to it that no one comes short
of the grace of God; that no root
of bitterness springing up cause
trouble, and by it many be defiled.*

HEBREWS 12:15 (NASB)

Pillows! They can be decorative or practical. They can lend support to an aching back or make a dull sofa look like new. The strategic use of pillows can provide an easy, inexpensive way to set a mood or tie together mismatched pieces with color.

Try tucking a standard-size bed pillow into a king-sized pillowcase and tying the extra fabric with silk cord or ribbon. You'll have a pretty pillow with flowering fabric at the ends—almost like a gift-wrapped package.

One thing is for sure—never skimp on your sleeping pillows. Is there anything more miserable than a stiff or lumpy pillow? No matter how pretty the pillowcase, it can't make up for a bad night's rest.

God says something similar about us. First Samuel 16:7 (NASB) says, "God sees not as man sees, for man looks at the outward appearance, but the LORD looks at the heart." Make sure that what's inside is just as pretty as what's outside. Our outward appearance is gift wrapping for the soul!

Simple Pleasures

- ...knowing you have a full tank of gas.
- ...two scoops instead of just one.
- ...clean windows that let the light of day shine through.

Wisdom for Living

Can You help me, Lord, to be authentic? I want what's on the inside to match what's on the outside. No more games, no more mere appearances.

Keys to Managing Time

I have set the Lord always before me: because he is at my right hand, I shall not be moved.

PSALM 16:8 (KJV)

Keys, keys. Keys to the car. Keys to the house. Keys to the locker at the sports club. Sometimes you can find your keys, and sometimes you can't. Here are three keys to help manage your time. Keep these handy, and you'll be surprised at how simple life can be!

Use a notebook for calendars and vital information. It will help you keep track of all your basic records and appointments.

Set a specific and regular time for organizing work. Divide up a complex problem into manageable segments. It may involve changing your habits, revising your schedule, or reorganizing your surroundings. You decide your best time to solve your problems. It's not how long you spend on a task, but how effective you are.

Identify a small group of projects—rank them by number according to how aggravating they are! A problem causing serious tension is a *one,* and one that would wait until next month is a *ten.*

Now go ahead—reward yourself with a little time, just for you!

Simple Pleasures

- Go ahead and lick the batter bowl. Heaven!
- Schedule a time to have the house to yourself for even a couple of hours.
- Do something fun with a tax refund.

Wisdom for Living

*Oh, the frustrations of life! God, I want to be a testimony
to Your peace and joy, and yet I am so anxious at times. Just now,
calm my spirit. My hope is in You.*

Making the Most of Leftovers

Who then is that faithful and wise steward, whom his lord shall make ruler over his household, to give them their portion of meat in due season?

LUKE 12:42 (KJV)

If you're raising a busy family, leftovers are a part of daily living! If you've lived life for 20 or 30 years, you know that leftovers are a way of life. Being good stewards of our resources means making the most of what we have—even leftovers.

When you have a few crumbs left in a bag of potato chips or box of crackers, save them. Lightly coat them with butter and toast them in the oven until brown. They make a tasty topping for casseroles or baked vegetables.

Bake six large potatoes. Eat them baked the first night. Then dice the leftovers, and fry them up in a bit of butter. They're wonderful for breakfast with eggs and bacon. The last two potatoes can be cubed and serve in a cream sauce with some cheese. Delicious!

Do you have some cooked meat left over? Chop it into pieces, add a tiny amount of mayonnaise, bell pepper, and celery, and you have a salad spread for sandwiches.

Making good use of leftover food can leave you with some "leftover" time! Use this for the important things in life!

Simple Pleasures

- Pull out a flannel nightgown and snuggle in early.
- Turn off the phone so you don't hear it ring for a quiet evening.
- Set your alarm a little earlier so you can transition slowly into the day.

Wisdom for Living

Life's short, Lord. Help me not to waste a thing!

A Special Golden Rule

> I will make your battlements of rubies, your gates of sparkling jewels, and all your walls of precious stones.
>
> ISAIAH 54:12

We've lived for a long time by a very special golden rule. It's one that will fit everybody and make the home a more special place to live: Have nothing in your house that you do not know to be useful or believe to be beautiful. Our homes need to be both practical and aesthetically pleasing. Practical for living, beautiful for pleasure.

Let's start with the most utilitarian objects in your home—file cabinets, refrigerators, and built-in cabinetry. These items can be refurbished, painted, stained, and decorated. You don't have to stick with the look you started with.

Give kitchen cabinets a facelift with a simple coat of paint—distress, crackle, stencil, or stamp them. Or replace the handles—you'll be surprised at the difference it makes.

Finally, give your work spaces a facelift. You'll reap a double benefit for a single sowing. First, you reap the joy of working in a wonderful room. Second, you'll reap the fruit of the creative work you do there for your family.

Simple Pleasures

Taste is made up of three things—
education, sensibility, and morality.

—RUSSELL LYNES

Wisdom for Living

Gracious heavenly Father, I humble myself before You today and ask that You will remake those areas of my life that need to look more like You. I trust You to direct my steps.

Excuse This House

> For whosoever shall do the will of God, the same is my brother, and my sister, and mother.
>
> MARK 3:35 (KJV)

I share this wonderful poem to remind us all that it's not what people see that matters most, but what most people never see. It puts the simple things of our lives into perspective.

Excuse This House!

Some houses try to hide the fact that children live there.
Ours boasts of it quite openly. The signs are everywhere.
For smears are on the windows, little smudges on the doors;
I should apologize I guess—for toys strewn on the floor.
But I sat down with the children—and we played and laughed and
    read.
And if the doorbell doesn't shine, their eyes will shine instead.
For when at times I'm forced to choose the one job or the other,
I want to be a housewife—but first I'll be a mother.

—AUTHOR UNKNOWN

Don't you love that? It's such a simple truth! And it's something we can all apply.

Simple Pleasures

Friendship always benefits...

—LUCIUS ANNAEUS SENECA

Wisdom for Living

Heavenly Father, give me the strength this day to minister to those around me. Some need firmness, some need kindness, some need a listening ear. Give me the gift of discernment, dear Lord.

Dreaming on a Tiny Budget

> For the Lord God is a sun and shield; the Lord gives grace and glory; no good thing does He withhold from those who walk uprightly.
>
> PSALM 84:11 (NASB)

Being realistic can be a very spiritual exercise. We have to exercise faith to look life straight in the eye at times and declare, "This is the way it is!" Other times though, the right response is to look beyond those limitations and dream about how life is meant to be lived. Dear lady, today don't let a tiny budget keep you from dreaming.

If you love a custom look, but don't have a custom budget, consider a "semi-designer" approach. Use a professional to help you get the right pieces, then decorate the rest of the room on your own. Enjoy the process. You'll get there.

Baskets, quilts, musical instruments, tools, and collections all have wonderful design possibilities. And don't overlook your children's art! It's an untapped source of decorating treasure. Frame a series of crayon drawings in matching frames and hang them as a group on your kitchen or hallway wall. Not only will you have unique and original art on your walls, but it will be an encouragement to your children as well.

Break free from the prison of thinking that it has to match! Who said that it does? Have fun being creative. Even if you can't dream big, dream!

Simple Pleasures

Little minds are interested in the extraordinary;
great minds in the commonplace.

—ELBERT HUBBARD

Wisdom for Living

O God, Your simple, majestic love is enough for me today. Help me sort through my priorities so that they might reflect Your dreams for me.

All Dressed Up

Enter His gates with thanksgiving, and His courts with praise. Give thanks to Him; bless His name.

PSALM 100:4 (NASB)

If you want your living space to be comfortable and welcoming to everyone who lives there, why not try including them in the process of planning and decorating?

Be prepared, however. It may mean you have to alter your dream of a dainty wicker and chintz sitting room to accommodate your husband's dream of an old leather easy chair, or even throw a couple of bean bags in the family room for your children, but the result will be more comfortable for everyone.

Involve a friend by asking her to help you choose the right fabric for a window covering, help you hang pictures, or even start a furniture refinishing project together—then return the favor. Your home should be fun for you, too, and not taking it all so seriously is sometimes just the thing to do.

Finally, try "dressing" your house for the change of seasons. It will give you *and* your house a change of pace! There are so many things you can do to capture the joy of the holidays, the beauty of the spring, the warmth of the fall. Children love to be a part of this as well, and it calls attention the beautiful world our Creator has made.

Simple Pleasures

- Hang a rod above your bed. Drape it with pretty fabric for a classic look.
- Experiment with fragrance—on yourself, or in your home, bath, or bed.
- Try this simple dressing: Mix four tablespoons olive oil to one of vinegar, add salt and shallots, and spread lightly on lettuce.

Wisdom for Living

Father, help me with my motives. Purify me, Lord, and I will be pure.

Celebrate Everything

Oh give thanks to the Lord, for He is good; for His lovingkindness is everlasting.

PSALM 107:1 (NASB)

Make celebrations a tradition in your family! Why not? Life is for living, and in the living there's always something to celebrate.

Celebrate everything—good days, bad days that are finally over, birthdays, and even non-birthdays! Get your children involved preparing for a dinner celebration. Make it special. Let them make place cards, set the table, help you cook, or create the centerpiece.

Our children were always assigned to greet guests at the door and take their coats—a wonderful opportunity for teaching hospitality and manners.

Let your sharing extend beyond your family. Several times a year, create a "love basket" filled with food for a needy family. Or try spending part of your holidays helping out a shelter or a mission.

Buy a "Special Person" plate and use it at meals to say "We love you" to a member of the family.

Don't be limited. Look for ways to celebrate life and those you love!

Simple Pleasures

- Luxuriate in a steamy tub laced with fresh sprigs of rosemary.
- Rise early and head out for a long walk at the beach.
- Invite a few friends over for a potluck dinner, or cook the meal together.

Wisdom for Living

Heavenly Father, there are a million reasons to celebrate today. Let me be a helper for those who want to celebrate, but don't know how.

The Tiny Touches

God saw all that he had made,
and it was very good. And there
was evening, and there was
morning—the sixth day.

Have you ever noticed how the tiny touches can make such a big difference? This is true in just about everything we do. It's true of the world God created as well.

Look for ways to add a tiny touch today to all you do. It's a way of saying, "I worship a God who cares about the details," for He truly does.

Tonight, instead of just plopping the tub of butter on the table, try putting your whipped butter in a white crock. Instead of putting the mustard and ketchup containers on your pretty table, try using a small bowl with a spoon. These simplest of things say to those you love, "We have time; let's care for each other."

One of my favorite things to do is to use tiny jam jars as flower vases. I love to set these at each person's place for breakfast or near where I know my son or daughter will do their studying.

Birthday or not, everyone loves a present. Often I place a tiny gift by our dinner plates—a little book, or a pen—something each person will like.

Look around. God has added His tiny touches everywhere. Do you see them?

Simple Pleasures

- Pause over a cup of tea to look at flower and seed catalogs.
- Select a gardening smock to be a part of your gardening ritual.
- Prepare a strategy for spring cleaning.

Wisdom for Living

I'm so grateful that details matter to You, Lord.
Your work is a delight to my soul.

The Games Children Play

Neither count I my life dear unto myself, so that I might finish my course with joy...to testify to the gospel of the grace of God.

ACTS 20:24 (KJV)

One of the great privileges of being a parent or a grandparent is to provide a nurturing, healthy environment for our children. Here are some ideas to encourage you to keep it simple, and to make your home a child-friendly zone!

Let your play time with your children be a time when you can let your hair down, too. You will be surprised by how deeply children are touched when adults come down to their level. In fact, every once in a while, modify the rules of a game so that all ages can participate. Even adults can still enjoy a good old-fashioned game of tag, hide-and-seek, or kick the can. Relax and have fun.

Before you relegate a piece of old clothing or jewelry to the garage sale stack, stop and think: Would this work in a dress-up box? Could my children have some fun with this? Children love to play with adults' stuff.

When you spend time with your children, make it fun and carefree. What we share with our children—time together, God's Word, and playful games—they will share with generations to come.

Simple Pleasures

- Find a hat that suits you and wear it proudly.
- Take a child on a walk near a lake or pond. Feed the ducks.
- Play "shopping" with children and talk to them as though they were adults.

Wisdom for Living

I pray for the children I know today, heavenly Father. Watch over them, care for them. Draw them closer to You. By Your Spirit, impress upon them Your great love for them.

Loving Children Makes for Loving Children

Moses therefore wrote this song the same day, and taught it the children of Israel.

DEUTERONOMY 31:22 (KJV)

Showing your love for children can be so simple. The wonderful reward will be children that are truly loving children to you, to their siblings, and to their friends. It starts with creating a life and a home that is child-friendly.

The good news is that it doesn't have to be expensive! Wonderful, usable toys can be found at garage sales, discount stores, or even in your attic. Even at retail price, classic toys such as dominoes, blocks, and cuddly stuffed animals are remarkably inexpensive.

If you're in doubt about how to equip your child-friendly home, invite a child to advise you. Buy what tickles your memories, what triggers warm, cozy feelings, what tempts you to get down on the floor and play. Buy something that makes you happy, and then look for a child to share it with.

These special and very precious moments with your children or grandchildren are wonderful opportunities to tell them how much you love them—and how much their heavenly Father cares for them and loves them too!

Simple Pleasures
- Send an invitation to three little girls and invite them to your home for a tea party.
- Make tiny, buttonlike tarts to accompany your tea.
- Place a small vase at each place filled with tiny flowers.

Wisdom for Living
Thank You, Father, for loving little children. Give me Your heart toward them so that they will be able to see Your great love through me.

Promises to Keep

God did this so that...we who have fled to take hold of the hope offered to us may be greatly encouraged.

HEBREWS 6:18

I know you know this, but here's a reminder: Don't make promises if you're not going to keep them. Most people would rather not have a promise than have one that isn't kept.

Husbands love wives who keep their promises. Children love it when parents promise a special outing and it actually comes to pass. Friends value someone who does what she says, someone who can be counted on.

People will be pleasantly surprised when you keep your promises. As a friend of mine says, "It takes so little to be above average!" When you develop a reputation for being a woman who does what she says, your life will have more meaning, and people will enjoy being around you.

Proverbs 20:7 (NASB) says, "A righteous [woman] who walks in [her] integrity—how blessed are [her] sons after [her]." It's really so simple, and it makes your life more effective—be committed to fulfilling what you've uttered.

Truly, keeping promises reflects on our Christian witness. Carry out today the promises you made yesterday!

Simple Pleasures

* Anticipate the performance of nature.
* Gather your blessings and offer a bouquet of thanksgiving to God.
* Create comfortable settings that invite intimacy.

Wisdom for Living

Holy, holy, holy, Lord God Almighty. You are perfect in power and in love.

Create in me a clean heart, O
God; and renew a right spirit
within me.

PSALM 51:10 (KJV)

We all need to nourish our creative potential. Human beings are expressive creatures by nature. So let's have some fun today with decorating! Let's see if we can discover the unique style that you can call your own. How do you discover your own unique style? Here are some tips.

The first thing you want to do is to look around in all the shops you can't afford. That sounds like fun, doesn't it? Visit some model homes. Take notes. Make little drawings. Then pick up a variety of decorating magazines.

Once you get back home, the real fun begins. Grab a cup of tea, find a comfy corner, and have a ball with the magazines you brought home. Pull out pages that appeal to you and set them aside. Once you've finished with your materials, then take a look at what you've selected. I'll bet you've discovered something about yourself. Remember, style isn't what you have, it's what you *do* with what you have!

Make your home uniquely *you*. Create a place where you can close the door on a busy day and enjoy a time for you and the Lord!

Simple Pleasures

* What are your favorite books? Reread several of them.
* Grab your spouse or friend and go out to a different restaurant once a week.
* Splurge on opera or theater tickets.

Wisdom for Living

Heavenly Father, I know I need less than I think I need. Stir up the creative spirit You've placed within me, and show me how to find You in the simple and ordinary things of my day.

Decorating Gold

Choose for yourselves this day whom you will serve....But as for me and my household, we will serve the Lord.

JOSHUA 24:15

Something old, something new, something borrowed...it's not just for weddings! It's also the secret to decorating beautifully on a budget.

If you want a rich look on a not-so-rich budget, shop by what I call the 25-75 rule. Is that new to you? Let me explain.

When you put the 25-75 rule into practice, the bulk of your décor—75 percent—can come from very inexpensive sources. It can even be of lesser quality.

However, to make the rule work, the 75 percent has to be balanced with a few pieces of real, lasting quality. At least 25 percent of your furnishings and accessories should be of quality workmanship—a beautiful oak chair, a print of fine art, or a lovely bed. This 25 percent will balance off the discount-store linens and the junk-shop mirror.

The secret to shopping without depleting your budget is learning to find decorating gold in the least likely places. Isn't this just how our heavenly Father looks at us? We are *decorating gold!*

Simple Pleasures

- Buy savings bonds. Give them as gifts to your grandchildren.
- Sit still and let yourself think for a moment.
- Take a car trip with a friend—it's the best way to enjoy long talks.

Wisdom for Living

Father, You are the gold in my life, my treasure. Teach me to care for the life of Your Spirit within me. Teach me how to nurture my walk with You.

A Simple Piece of Cloth

If God so clothe the grass of the field, which to day is, and to morrow is cast into the oven, shall he not much more clothe you, O ye of little faith?

MATTHEW 6:30 (KJV)

Here are a few ideas to make fabric finds go a long way.

Should you hem it, add ribbons to it, or simply tie it onto a curtain rod for a quick decorative look at that blasé bathroom window?

Maybe its pretty print would be best draped over a small side table or nightstand. Better yet, maybe it is the perfect complement to your table service pattern. Cut it into fourths, hem each part, and you have four beautiful napkins.

Some other uses? They are limitless. How about taking your pinking or fringing shears to the edges and using the fabric to line drawers or baskets or to paper the interior of a cabinet? Wrap a present or cover a cardboard box for pretty storage.

And here's another simple truth for you today: When your day is hemmed with prayer, it's less likely to unravel!

Simple Pleasures

* Light your fireplace for breakfast—the glow will stay with you all day.
* Soup is the perfect comfort food. Serve it in a beautiful tureen.
* Buy a chair to call your own.

Wisdom for Living

Lord, let me rest in the reality of Your presence and
Your promised guidance. As the Scripture says,
"You surround me with songs of deliverance."

The Secret of Little Bags

Though thy beginning was small,
yet thy latter end should greatly
increase.

JOB 8:7 (KJV)

Bite-size pieces. That's how I've managed to find my way to life and home organization—by taking it one step at a time, little by little. One of the most simple ideas I've discovered to aid my organizational efforts is to use my "little bags."

When I run out the door, I grab the various bags I need, and into my purse they go. One of my little bags holds my sunglasses. One of my little makeup bags holds a mirror, lipstick, a small comb, blush, and a nail file. The other one holds cosmetics for a quick touch-up.

In addition to my wallet, sunglasses bag, and makeup bag, I have a little bag for reading glasses and two more for various items. You can even designate a bag for business cards, seldom-used credit cards, a tea bag, and Sweet 'n' Low. Find out what works for you.

The whole idea is to create more time for you—more time to read a favorite book, time to stop and notice a garden flower, time to spend quietly with the Lord. Precious moments help to make life work!

Simple Pleasures

* Enjoy those quiet moments throughout the day when you are alone.
* Play a CD of Broadway tunes and dance your way around the house.
* Many libraries have art you can check out—a wonderful way to learn.

Wisdom for Living

You value the little things in life, Lord. I want Your heart,
and I know that this means slowing down enough to see life from Your
perspective. Help me to grow little by little, as Your Word says.

The "Barnes Barn" Is His

Therefore, since we receive a kingdom which cannot be shaken, let us show gratitude...

HEBREWS 12:28 (NASB)

As much as my husband, Bob, and I love our home, we believe that it belongs to God, not to us. In fact, six weeks after we moved into our Barnes Barn, we invited some friends and our pastor to dinner.

After dinner, we had a little ceremony dedicating our house and the property to God. We walked into each room and prayed a blessing upon its walls, asking that peace, joy, love, honesty, and patience would permeate the surroundings.

I believe our home has been a rich source of blessing to us and to others over the years. We've had dinners, Bible studies, and many other wonderful gatherings in our Barn.

Allow the joy and peace of our Lord to permeate the walls of your home as well as the "rooms" of your life. Let Him have access to every nook and cranny. Open your heart to that spirit of loveliness that only Christ Himself can give you.

Simple Pleasures
I love things that bear the touch of time, chips and all—
they are more beautiful than perfection.

—*VICTORIA MAGAZINE*

Wisdom for Living
*Yes, Lord, permeate every area of my life with Your goodness,
Your truth, and Your love, so that my life might be a blessing to others.
Let Your blessings lead them to You.*

May

THE ART OF LINGERING

It Takes Time to Save Time

All over the world this gospel is bearing fruit and growing, just as it has been doing among you since the day you heard it and understood God's grace in all its truth.

COLOSSIANS 1:6

Do you want to find greater simplicity in every area of your life? Start by breaking the chronic procrastinator's habit. Whenever you catch yourself thinking "I don't have time now; I'll do it later," stop—and do it now.

Before you begin, take the important step of asking yourself, "Is there an easier or better way to do this?" If you're like me, sometimes this is the most difficult moment, because I want to get on to the next thing. It requires discipline and patience to do it right the first time.

It isn't always important to wait until you have time to finish the entire task. Some tasks must be broken down into smaller steps. Do what you can now, do it correctly, and come back to it later to finish up. On the other hand, don't get so many projects going that you never finish anything.

Build toward having more time in the future by making wise decisions today. Each moment of your life, once gone, is lost forever. Think of time invested today as time saved tomorrow. Start making time for the important things in life!

Simple Pleasures

Now the bright Morning star, day's harbinger,
Comes dancing from the East and brings
with her the flowery May.

—JOHN MILTON, "MAY SONG"

Wisdom for Living

Lord, I am so grateful that You are teaching me to order my days and to apply my heart to wisdom. Guide my steps along Your pathways this day.

The Children in Our Lives

*He who fears the
secure fortress, a
it will be a refuge.*

Nurturing healthy children includes caring about the simple things that make up a day. I hope some of these ideas will be helpful.

When a child is upset or out of control, try "time outs." This means moving your child to a designated chair or area for a brief period (one minute for every year of age is a good rule) to cool off. It will give him or her—and you—a chance to regroup.

Define boundaries and show your child how far he or she may go.

Include children—even the youngest—in the housework or the chores around the yard. Make the jobs age-appropriate. For example, an hour of work is about all you can expect from an eight-year-old.

God wants us to see each one of our children as a delicate rose—eager to unfold its petals to the sun. Remember, once those petals are torn off by harsh words, criticism, or anger, it's almost impossible to put them back on again. Be gentle today, even as the Lord is gentle with you.

Simple Pleasures

* Feel the comfort of hearing your cat purr.
* Notice the differences in the dawn depending on the season.
* Enjoy memories that come while eating a peanut butter and jelly sandwich.

Wisdom for Living

*With a child's heart, I come to You, Father, and
surrender myself to You this day. Thank You for Your tenderness
and gentleness toward me. You are my life!*

The Ingredients of Home

And let the beauty of the Lord our God be upon us: and establish thou the work of our hands upon us; yea, the work of our hands establish thou it.

PSALM 90:17 (KJV)

What's the first thing that pops into your mind when you think of *home?* Here are some great ideas to help your home to create pleasant memories.

A bright banner hanging by your door will say "Hello, you're welcome" to everyone who comes. In fact, have one for every season of the year! Or, if you're really bold, paint the front door bright red! Home is a place where we express ourselves.

Home is a place of good smells. Think of your favorites, and plan to share these with your family and friends whenever the occasion arises. Baking cookies, roasting turkey, brewing coffee—these smells and so many others make us feel at home.

Here's one of my favorite recipes. Wow! What a wonderful, welcoming aroma you'll produce with this—and you'll have dinner to boot! Give it a try! Marinate a cut-up chicken in fresh orange juice, two cloves crushed garlic, sliced ginger root, and one tablespoon Worcestershire sauce. Bake slowly for two hours at 250 degrees.

Simple Pleasures

Wait not until tomorrow;
Gather the roses of life today.

—PIERRE DE RONSARD

Wisdom for Living

The sights, the sounds, the smells of home...as I put my hands to the tasks of homemaking, may all I do be unto You, my Strength and my Redeemer.

The Lord's curse is on the house of the wicked, but he blesses the home of the righteous.

PROVERBS 3:33

God is the Creator, and He's in the business of creating even today. Let His creativity shine through you as you create your home. It's really a lot easier than you think to add creative touches here and there as you allow Him to show you the way.

Who would have thought that a bedsheet could be used in so many ways! The first time I used a bedsheet as a tablecloth, everyone thought it was a little strange. Today, however, sheets are used for curtains, drapes, sofa cushions, wallpaper, and much, much more.

A friend of mine took Ralph Lauren sheets she bought on sale and decorated her entire house in the same print, a beautiful blue floral. She even put the fabric in her kitchen cupboards. How creative!

With a spirit of creativity you can put together a homey environment out of whatever you have. Remember, the key is to keep it simple. Proverbs tells us that a woman's "worth is far above jewels." Each of us can find new sources of creativity as we trust the Creator to enable us, and to give us the courage to step out.

Simple Pleasures

- Take a lovers' stroll through a meadow or wooded forest.
- Velvety red roses still symbolize love.
- Put a note on the bathroom mirror that will make your loved one smile.

Wisdom for Living

May righteousness be the first ingredient of my godly home, dear Lord. May my life be a living sacrifice to You.

Kitchen Fellowship

May my prayer be set before you like incense; may the lifting up of my hands be like the evening sacrifice.

PSALM 141:2

Does your life say "Welcome" to those you come in contact with, or does it say something a little less warm and friendly like "Stay Out!"? What people sense on the outside can be a true reflection of life on the inside. That is certainly something to think about today!

Our kitchens can tell us a lot about our homes as well. Are they places that say, "Life is happening here!" or do they shout out something less inviting, like "Disaster zone! Caution!"? Here are some ideas for creating the kind of kitchen and home you desire.

Help a child plant some seeds in a small container, and place it in your kitchen window to sprout.

Instead of buying regular applesauce, buy apples. A bowl of homemade applesauce with a sprinkle of cinnamon is an easy-to-make snack or dessert.

Stir up a batch of blueberry or cranberry muffins for a sweet and colorful treat.

Make a habit of inviting God to be present at your meals. Stop, hold hands, and ask the Lord's blessing on the meal—and on those gathered around the table. It's as simple as that.

Simple Pleasures

- Use calligraphy to personalize your notes and invitations.
- Look for something in your day that is truly beautiful.
- Shop a few garage sales this weekend, and see what treasures you find.

Wisdom for Living

Father, thank You for the gift of food. Oh, how we love to eat good food prepared by loving hands. What a good God You are to consider all our needs.

Start Early

My soul waiteth for the Lord more than they that watch for the morning: I say, more than they that watch for the morning.

PSALM 130:6 (KJV)

The early morning hours are some of the best times to accomplish those very *daily* tasks. Something about the cool morning air can make it all seem a little more enjoyable. The Bible admonishes us to begin early, and this principle applies to children as well. Yes, children need to be organized, too.

Start early to delegate household chores. Rotate the chores to keep them interesting. Review the family calendar together so that you're ready for the week with the least amount of surprises. At least once a month, invite the children to the kitchen to prepare a meal. Desserts are always a winner.

Setting a few rituals in place really works well with children. One of our family favorites was the old cowbell by the kitchen door. Two minutes before a meal, I'd ring it—very firmly. It let my children (and husband) know that they had two minutes to get to the table.

One of the most valuable gifts you can give your children is to teach them how to work and what it means to hear the words "well done." Start early!

Simple Pleasures

- Begin to prepare your vegetable garden by turning the soil.
- Develop a simple site map that will guide your garden planting.
- Select seeds for your garden and interesting stakes to mark the rows.

Wisdom for Living

I love Your mornings, Father. Your mercies are new every day. When I awake, I am still with You. Take me into this new day.

Praying for Friends

It is of the Lord's mercies that we are not consumed, because his compassions fail not. They are new every morning: great is thy faithfulness.

LAMENTATIONS 3:22-23 (KJV)

As you drive to work, pray for a friend. As you wait in the grocery line, pray for a friend. Pray for your friends when you're stuck in traffic, or when your child runs crying from the room because of some frustration or heartbreak. Pray for wisdom for your friends who have children—they might be going through the same kind of thing.

Colossians 1:9-12 is a wonderful model for prayer. Look at what you'll be asking God: That your friend will have spiritual wisdom and understanding; that she will walk in a manner worthy of the Lord, pleasing to Him in all respects; that your friend will be bearing fruit in all good work, and increasing in the knowledge of God; and that she will be strengthened with all power, for the attaining of all steadfastness and patience.

What an armor of protection and growth you can give your friend with a prayer like that! And don't limit this prayer to friends. This is an excellent model in prayer for your husband and members of your family as well. Let me tell you—it's a real comfort to have a friend praying for me!

Simple Pleasures

A final comfort that is small but not cold: The heart is the only broken instrument that works.

—T.E. KALEN

Wisdom for Living

Father, I entrust my friendships and my friends to You. They are gifts in my life. I humbly call on You to bless them this day and to draw them closer to You.

Know Your Child

Hear, O my
sayings; and
shall be many
instruction; le
her; for she is

Enter

When Bob and I were raising our own children, Jenny and Brad, we saw many differences between them. We soon came to realize that each child had his or her own bent, and that this was already established when God placed these two special people in our family.

God has given you a unique child as well. Get to know him or her. Write down in your journal the ways your children are different. Take time to think through the way your training will differ from child to child based on their own unique temperaments, life experiences, and even their position in the family.

Learn one new thing about each of your children today. Then, take that insight and use it to encourage, correct, or instruct. Find a quiet moment to share a special memory or event with your child.

The important thing is to praise your child today for being uniquely made. Proverbs 22:6 says it ever so simply: "Train a child in the way he should go, and when he is old he will not turn from it."

Simple Pleasures

- Listen to National Public Radio.
- Watch your kids while they are sleeping.
- Notice when the days start to get a little longer.

Wisdom for Living

*Lord, one of the children in my life needs You so desperately.
What can I do to help? Thank You, Jesus, that You intercede for us at the
right hand of the Father. I bring this child before You.*

aining or ospitality?

Many of us love to entertain! It's always great fun to plan our menu, gather together our ingredients, set a beautiful table, select our centerpiece, and anticipate a wonderful time together. Unfortunately, by the time our guests arrive, we are often too stressed and exhausted to offer them what they need most—our loving attention.

The Bible talks about something quite different from mere entertaining. We can entertain as much as we like, but not until we *care* does it become hospitality.

One busy working mom I know discovered the way to fast, convenient hospitality. She'd pick up a bunch of flowers and frozen lasagna. At home, she baked the lasagna in one of her own casserole dishes, tossed a prepared salad in a pretty wooden bowl, brought out frozen cake for dessert, and lit a candle. Within moments she served a lovely dinner. No one knew she didn't work for hours preparing the meal.

What she offered her friends was a chance to see Jesus in her calm and loving home. And she had the opportunity to touch their lives with her spirit of joy and caring. Try offering hospitality—people will always come back for more!

Simple Pleasures

* Purchase an art book. Spend time looking through it with a friend.
* Let a candle burn in your entryway as a sign of warmth and welcome.
* Give something of your own to a child you love.

Wisdom for Living

Lord, this is it. I'm having company for dinner and I want to stay calm.
Help me trust You with the outcome. Grace me to attend to my guests.
I want them to be comfortable.

An Enjoyable Place

Only one thing is needed. Mary has chosen what is better, and it will not be taken away from her.

LUKE 10:42

Our kitchen should and can be an enjoyable place! The secret is in learning to do things the simplest way possible.

First, unclutter your life. Get rid of clutter. It will give you more room to work, and it makes cleaning so much easier. Keep stacks from collecting on counters and tables. I find that one or two "kitchen overflow" boxes come in handy.

Store items like picnic utensils, holiday stuff, and extra plates and dishes in the garage, or even under a bed. Items that are used seasonally don't need to be visible the rest of the year, and storing them elsewhere keeps drawers and cupboards from becoming cluttered.

If your kitchen's drab and boring, spruce it up! Fresh paint, a few flowers, or even a candle does wonders. Make your kitchen the place to be. Make it fun and enjoyable. Make it the "heart" of your home.

Proverbs 31:27 is a great reminder: "She watches over the affairs of her household...."

Simple Pleasures

When I was young, we always had mornings like this.

—A.A. MILNE

Wisdom for Living

Strengthen me for the tasks before me. I want to be faithful, Lord. I want to hear You say to me, "Well done, good and faithful servant." You are my strength.

Give thanks unto the Lord, call upon his name, make known his deeds among the people.

1 CHRONICLES 16:8 (KJV)

Do you expect too much of yourself and others? I think I sometimes do. One of the things I've had to learn over the years is to find ways to save time and money, and then not let myself feel guilty, as if I short-changed anyone along the way. What's important is to have time for what really counts!

Save time and money with one-dish salad meals. Combine diced left-over meat, fish, or poultry with fresh vegetables. Use leftovers as snacks or for lunch, or freeze them to use another time.

Turn a simple pasta side dish into a meal by serving it with a salad. Try to include "filling" food on your menus for the hearty eaters in your family. Chili, stew, sandwiches, and crockpot dishes are great choices. Make your own salad dressing. Use water instead of milk for scrambled eggs or omelets—it makes them fluffier.

The bottom line is to enjoy your mealtimes. Do your best on the food, and then take a few minutes when you're all together to have each person read a verse from the Bible. Pray and thank the Lord for the bounty in your life!

Simple Pleasures

- Hang your basket collection from the walls of your breakfast room.
- Make tiny dollar pancakes for a Saturday morning treat.
- Spread out a checkered tablecloth on the floor and have a picnic.

Wisdom for Living

Praise the Lord. Praise His holy name.
Let all that hath breath praise the Lord.

Appetites of the Heart

With good will render service, as to the Lord, and not to men.

EPHESIANS 6:7 (NASB)

God made us to need the nourishment of food. We all like different things, but we all need the same things to function properly—vitamins, minerals, fruits and vegetables, grains, and milk products. We all need fuel to live our daily lives.

Kitchens are wonderful and irresistible places for children—and ours were in the kitchen from the time they were tiny. Now it's our grandchildren! Children need to be in the kitchen, not only because it's a center of family warmth, but also because they need to learn kitchen skills—to measure and stir, to read recipes, and to plan meals.

There's no doubt about it; this can be a messy proposition. But children are washable—and so is your kitchen. I consider the extra cleanup time to be a worthwhile investment in a future of happy kitchen hours for myself and for this next generation.

While you're nourishing their bodies, don't forget to nourish their spirits. Talk to them about the great Bible stories or work on memorizing a verse or two. Our homes are places of refreshment—for the body and for the spirit.

Simple Pleasures

- Serve your children breakfast in bed with some of their favorite foods.
- Offer up a delectable appetizer of sliced pear and a sharp cheese.
- Dip a plump strawberry in powdered sugar and savor a bit of sunshine.

Wisdom for Living

Dear Lord, I so need You today. My spirit feels dry and lifeless. Nourish me, Father. Feed me by Your Spirit and through the truth of Your Word.

Toy Centers

*Be glad in the Lord, and rejoice,
ye righteous: and shout for joy, all
ye that are upright in heart.*

PSALM 32:11 (KJV)

It's so simple to delight a child. Use your imagination and you'll be delighted, too. Try this and see!

Children love to pretend and imagine and create. Around our house, we have created what we call "toy centers"—places where kids can congregate and find lots of things to entertain and amuse them. One of these centers is upstairs in a loft. Another one at my home is in our breakfast area.

In the toy center, one of the favorite activities is to explore the fabric-covered box that they know is theirs. It's always there, ready for play. What's inside the box? Quiet activities to amuse children who might come with mom for a visit: a supply of crayons, coloring books, and simple games.

In my pantry and refrigerator (or freezer), I try to designate an area for child-friendly snacks: juice, peanut butter, fruit wraps, and popsicles.

It doesn't take much (really) to make your home child-friendly. Think of the dividends it will bring!

Simple Pleasures

- Let your grandchildren color a simple cardboard box for their own things.
- Bowling, a movie, miniature golf, or a video arcade are all fun for kids.
- Bake a batch of brownies together and send some over to a neighbor.

Wisdom for Living

*Restore unto me a childlike heart, Father.
You have given me everything I need for life and godliness.
Let me enter into life with abundance and with joy!*

There Is Always Room for "Thank You"

For Thou, O Lord, hast made me glad by what Thou hast done, I will sing for joy at the works of Thy hands.

PSALM 92:4 (NASB)

Saying "thank you" makes everybody feel a little bit happier. And it's so important for children to develop the wonderful habit of gratitude early in their lives.

Sometimes it's enough to just say the simple "thank you" in the same moment that something special happens. But if someone has sent a gift or done something especially nice for your child, an in-person "thank you" just isn't enough. Your child should also send that person a written thank-you note. These are wonderful opportunities to teach your child the importance of gratitude and how to best show it.

Thank-you notes can be bought or made. A drawing or a folded card they have made themselves gives them a chance to express their feelings from the heart. A sweet gift for your child could even be some note paper with their name stenciled on it—to use just for thank yous.

Of course, the side benefit in diligently teaching children to say "thank you" is that it will be so much easier in life for them to recognize the special gifts that God bestows each day, and to lift a grateful and thankful heart to their heavenly Father.

Simple Pleasures

Throughout life we hardly realize that we receive a great deal more than we give. It is only with gratitude that life becomes rich.

—DIETRICH BONHOEFFER

Wisdom for Living

Father, my heart is full of gladness at all Your wonderful blessings.
I want my mouth to speak Your praise as I go about this day.
All I have is from You.

The Beauty of Stewardship

He hath made every thing beautiful in his time: also he hath set the world in their heart, so that no man can find out the work that God maketh from the beginning to the end.

ECCLESIASTES 3:11 (KJV)

Stewardship. It's not a word we use very often. But it is an important word because it reminds us that we have resources that need to be well cared for.

Exercising our creativity is one way to be responsible stewards of the gifts and talents God has given us, and to rejoice in our identity as children made in His image. You can choose to be creative today—and every day! Discover the beauty of good stewardship.

Next time you shop the sales, buy a sheet in colors to match one of your rooms. Use it to cover a pillow or a wall—or make a curtain with it. Pick out some colorful ribbon. Tie different colors around your napkins; tuck a fresh flower under the ribbon. Make an everyday table extra special.

If you don't have a collection, start one! You'll have fun, and your family and friends will always know what to buy you. Pitchers, cookie jars, music boxes—the list is endless.

Stewardship of our creativity is simply this: making the ordinary, beautiful.

Simple Pleasures

- Dry clean or launder anything you're not going to wear for six months.
- Wood hangers are the best for hanging your best clothes.
- Clean a closet a day for a week. Next week, do drawers.

Wisdom for Living

You are making the ordinary beautiful in my life, dear God.
Help me not to take the ordinary for granted.
I know it is one of the most cherished gifts You give.

Togetherness

Praise ye the Lord. I will praise the Lord with my whole heart, in the assembly of the upright, and in the congregation.

PSALM 111:1 (KJV)

Is your home a place of *togetherness?* What can we do today that will encourage togetherness instead of working against it? Let's make "togetherness" happen today.

Little touches around your home can make a big difference. The way the furniture is arranged, for example, can tell a lot about your priorities. Are there comfortable groupings for conversation? Does every seat have an adequate lighting source and a place for each person to set their hot coffee or cold drink?

Another item to consider is the location of the television. Many family rooms these days are set up with every chair pointed at the TV. Small wonder that our society has a problem with TV addiction. I know some people who keep their TV on a wheeled cart in the closet, ready to roll out for special occasions, but safely stowed during ordinary family evenings.

Sitting and talking and playing and sharing our lives is what really matters. Such togetherness fills our homes with a warm fireside glow—with or without the fire!

Simple Pleasures

- Enjoy a lunch of grilled cheese sandwiches and tomato soup.
- Climb a mountain, or the nearest hill.
- Call your mother on the telephone.

Wisdom for Living

*Break down the walls that separate me from others, Lord.
I long for the intimacy that comes by Your Spirit.*

Everyday Welcome

I am not saying this because I am in need, for I have learned to be content whatever the circumstances.

PHILIPPIANS 4:11

Clutter wearies the spirit and fights against serenity. Have you noticed? So today, before you do anything else, take 15 minutes to dejunk the room where you spend your quiet time. If you don't finish today, take another 15 minutes tomorrow. Turn those private rooms in your house into places of welcome and refuge.

If your quiet place is your bedroom, then arrange the furniture so that the first thing you see as you enter the room is the bed. Cover it with a beautiful and inviting quilt or spread, pile it with pillows, and rejoice in the sense of welcome. Place some flowers on a table along with a selection of your favorite books. Give your spirit a reason to leap every time you enter the room.

For other decorating ideas, take 15 minutes to browse through the Bed and Bath section of a department store. Don't be afraid to adapt and copy! Everyone in the family will appreciate your efforts to create warm and cozy spaces.

Make your house a haven of beauty and serenity—a spiritual center, a true home.

Simple Pleasures

- Get plenty of sleep, so that you feel like getting up in the morning.
- Arrange a full day, so that you can hardly wait to go to bed at night.
- Enjoy a short nap sometime during the day.

Wisdom for Living

I'm going to unclutter my closets, my thoughts, my heart, and my life, Lord. It's time to make way for the new things You want to do in my life and my heart.

The Stillness of God

Make it your ambition to lead a quiet life, to mind your own business and to work with your hands, just as we told you.

1 THESSALONIANS 4:11

"Be still and know that I am God," the psalmist urges. Easier said than done, right? A recent report indicated that the noise level in our society is increasing, and with it comes a greater threat to our peace of mind and sanity. Seriously!

Stillness. It's not a word that many of us even use anymore, let alone experience. Yet we desperately need the spirit of stillness. We're constantly on the move. Constantly stretched to the max.

In order for the spirit of loveliness to live in us, we must seek out opportunities to rest, plan, regroup, and draw closer to God. With God's help, we can do whatever we really want to do, and we can make time for the really important things in our lives.

Each day, purposely set aside a few moments to make yourself unavailable to the world and available to God. These quiet times alone give Him a chance to reveal Himself to you, and ultimately, through you to others. The spirit of stillness is God's gift to you—a healing touch for your life.

Simple Pleasures

Fashion your own desert where you can
withdraw every day, shake off...compulsions, and
dwell in the gentle healing presence of our Lord.

—HENRI NOUWEN

Wisdom for Living

I am quiet before You. I long to hear Your voice. Speak, Lord.

Nooks and Crannies

When my glory passes by, I will put you in a cleft in the rock and cover you with my hand until I have passed by.

Exodus 33:22

Older homes have the advantage of having quaint little nooks and crannies. But you can create the same ambience in any home using cozy furniture and warm lighting. Children love nooks and crannies. They will make any child feel welcome in your home!

Children love spaces and furniture that are just their size—cozy little nooks where they curl up and play. I've yet to meet a child who could resist our loft. It's been a tea room, a game room, and a reading nook. We also keep a bunch of old dress-up clothes in the nook.

I'll never forget the day our grandson Chad came downstairs in my old blazer and a necktie from the dress-up closet, carrying a Bible. He announced in solemn tones that he was now a preacher!

You don't have to build a separate room in your home. A couple of child-sized rocking chairs in a cozy corner next to a basket of books will do it. Just *keep it simple!* It's all about nurturing our spirits and those of our children.

Simple Pleasures

* Arrange all your pictures in albums or organize them in shoe boxes.
* Give away some hugs today.
* After a disagreement, feel the peace of making up.

Wisdom for Living

It's time to cozy up into You, Lord. You have promised that if I draw near to You, You will draw near to me. I am drawing near, Lord. Thank You for drawing near to me.

Please Come for Tea

Whoever is thirsty, let him come; and whoever wishes, let him take the free gift of the water of life.

REVELATION 22:17

You don't have to be a little girl to love a tea party!

I love to serve afternoon guests fragrant cinnamon tea, poured into their choice from my cup and saucer collection, complemented with wonderful—and healthful—oatmeal cookies!

Try taking your hospitality on the road. Fill a basket with food and take it to someone in your church who needs encouragement—maybe a neighbor!

Many times I place a tiny gift by our dinner guests' plates. Everyone loves a present, even something small and simple.

What part of your home or apartment do you enjoy most? Let that aspect be the focus of your hospitality. Share what brings you pleasure.

And when someone entertains *you*, don't forget to thank them with a little note or a gift.

Don't miss the simple joy of sharing your Christian life through hospitality! When was the last time you said, "Please come for tea"?

Simple Pleasures

- Make kitchen counters inviting with a bowl of fruit or pretty pottery.
- A flower or candle by the sink will brighten the dishwashing task.
- An oversize clock in the kitchen is helpful and fun!

Wisdom for Living

*I want to be able to make others feel comfortable and welcome, Lord.
Will You grace me today with Your gifts of hospitality
so that I might be a blessing to others?*

Christmas in May

> Today in the town of David a Savior has been born to you; he is Christ the Lord.
>
> LUKE 2:11

Christmas. It's my favorite time of year! I love having friends and family over, hearing favorite carols on the radio, decorating the house from top to bottom in reds and greens. Every present is carefully picked and wrapped and hidden!

There are so many activities to enjoy, and all of them occurring in a few short weeks. Sometimes Christmas seems more about stress than spirit. With all the hustle and bustle, it's so easy to lose the true meaning of Christmas and wonder what happened by the time December twenty-fifth rolls around.

This year, why not start the season early and beat the commercial rush and pressure? Why not start thinking about Christmas in May? I've tried it now for several years, and the results have been wonderful.

In May, I start my master list of gifts to buy, menus to prepare, cookies to bake, and cards to send. When the season finally arrives, I enjoy it so much more. Christmas shouldn't be about stress. And it doesn't have to be.

Advance planning leaves you more time for the real meaning of Christmas!

Simple Pleasures

- Look through old December magazines for decorating ideas.
- Inventory your gift shelf to see what gifts still need to be purchased.
- Practice a new cookie recipe so you'll be ready when winter arrives.

Wisdom for Living

You came to us, dear Jesus, so long ago. I come to You today with open hands and an open heart. Teach me to praise Your name.

June

A Garden of Tranquillity

Be Still My Soul

Take my yoke upon you and learn from me, for I am gentle and humble in heart, and you will find rest for your souls.

MATTHEW 11:29

We make a big mistake if we forget to calm our spirits, and seek the stillness that each of us needs to walk at peace in this crazy world. The psalmist urged, "Be still, and know that I am God." Easier said than done, right?

The complaint I hear from so many women these days is, "I'm just dying for a little peace and quiet—a chance to relax, to think, and to pray."

Let me urge you today in the strongest possible terms: Do whatever it takes to nurture stillness in your life. Don't let the enemy wear you so thin that you lose your balance and perspective. Regular time for stillness is as important and necessary as sleep, exercise, and nutritious food.

So what's the secret to making the time you need for yourself? First, it helps to be realistic about what this will look like. It doesn't have to be a large block of time. Fifteen minutes here and there can do wonders.

Next, purpose to make yourself unavailable to the rest of the world for a few moments each day. Be available to God, to yourself, and then ultimately, to others.

Simple Pleasures

- Have breakfast by candlelight.
- Play a piece of quiet, classical music over lunch.
- Tonight, write a poem or record your thoughts in your journal.

Wisdom for Living

Lord, help me today to remember that You came to the world in a simple manger, to a simple man and woman. You came simply to love us. Thank You that all You ask of me is a simple response.

Pray Before You Plan

Unless the Lord builds the house, its builders labor in vain. Unless the Lord watches over the city, the watchmen stand guard in vain.

PSALM 127:1

Who you are will determine what your priorities are, and how your time will be apportioned. Interestingly, it also works the other way around. Your priorities will influence who you become, and will shape your life.

One very practical way of completing the awesome task of setting priorities is to list the things you have on your heart and mind to accomplish. Then, prayerfully consider each one's merit and timeliness. Arrange them in order of importance, and make any adjustments that come to mind as you seek to order your steps according to the Spirit's direction. Proceed as planned.

Managing your time well means finding God's focus for you—choosing a direction and moving ahead to accomplish your goals. Success in this area is one of the most difficult, yet it is a helpful skill a woman can develop. The Bible has laid the foundation, and it's so simple: "All things must be done properly and in an orderly manner" (1 Corinthians 14:40 NASB). Bless you today!

Simple Pleasures

- Take a train ride to the nearest large city; shop, have lunch, and return.
- Strike up a conversation with a stranger and give away a bit of joy.
- Clean up your bicycle and enjoy a tour around the neighborhood.

Wisdom for Living

Father, I move as Your Spirit leads me. Teach me not to move ahead or behind You, but at the impulse of Your leading within me.

Lead a quiet and peaceable life in all godliness and honesty. For this is good and acceptable in the sight of God our Saviour.

1 Timothy 2:2b-3 (kjv)

I love creating a space, no matter how small, that can help me organize my life. This is the place where I gather my thoughts, my materials, and my plans for realizing the life I am creating…with God's help and guidance. Here are a few simple ideas for creating your own personal work space in your home!

To help you choose that ideal setting, ask yourself these questions: Do you need a place where it's quiet? Or is it better to be near people? Do you prefer a sunny area or a shaded one? Do you prefer to work in the morning or the afternoon? The answer to these questions helps narrow your alternatives.

Walk around your home. See which areas meet the answers to your questions. Is there enough space for the computer? What about electrical outlets? Live with your selection a day or so and then get busy!

Being organized isn't the ultimate goal, but it does make life a bit easier. The point is that it gives you precious time for your family, your friends, and your church. These are the important things in life!

Simple Pleasures

- Give your residence a name that's meaningful to you. Then buy a porcelain or metal plaque to attach to the outside of the house. This is a wonderful European tradition that adds charm to any "cottage."

Wisdom for Living

I'm learning, Lord, and I'm so excited to see the changes in my life! You have promised to complete the work You began in me. I know Your Word is true.

Be a Blessing Today

Arise, shine, for your light has come, and the glory of the Lord rises upon you.

ISAIAH 60:1

One of my favorite verses is Song of Songs 2:12: "Flowers appear on the earth; the season of singing has come." What a simple truth for our lives. We often think that walking with the Lord has to entail something very big, something that seems eternally significant for God's kingdom. And yet, the flowers appear on the earth and raise their lovely heads in praise to the Lord.

Our lives are like that at times, aren't they? Have you ever felt dormant, like your life is in hibernation? Our spirits lie sleeping—forgotten, we think. Then something happens that makes us come forward, take a look at the sun, and decide we're going to be a blessing to someone today.

So let today be that day when you reach out, near or far, and bless someone. Make a phone call, write a letter, drop a note, send a gift. Record a blessing to someone on an audio tape and mail it to them.·

Don't put any expectations on your actions. Act out of pure love. Be like a "golden poppy" in someone's life. I think I hear singing!

Simple Pleasures

- Purchase a colorful cozy to continue a long tradition of tea rituals.
- Place white tulips in a glass bowl under a spotlight. Beautiful!
- Find a secret place in your garden where you can hide away.

Wisdom for Living

Shine Your light and Your love through me today, dear Lord.

The Motivations of Service

> Then Mary took about a pint of pure nard, an expensive perfume; she poured it on Jesus' feet and wiped his feet with her hair. And the house was filled with the fragrance of the perfume.
>
> JOHN 12:3

You have no doubt heard for most of your life, just as I have, that service is the real key to personal fulfillment. But there are many reasons and motivations behind the things people do for others. Let me encourage you today to look at your real motivation for serving!

I've often probed myself on this question: why do I serve? Matthew 20:14 has always intrigued me because of what it shows me about God. In this parable, the owner of the farm (who represents God, of course) says, "I want to give the man who was hired last the same pay as I gave these hired first!"

That philosophy is hard for some of us to swallow because it doesn't seem fair. But God chooses to do what He chooses to do. The question is, are we willing to serve God, not man?

Our reward is eternal life—even if we come to the field at three o'clock in the afternoon, and others have been there since early morning. Take a few minutes and write down ten blessings. You've been freely blessed. Be willing to freely serve!

Simple Pleasures

* Set off on a solitary stroll.
* Give blood at your local Red Cross blood bank.
* Offer to work in the nursery at church with the toddlers.

Wisdom for Living

Teach me to understand Your ways, dear Father. Your ways are higher than my ways. My heart desires to do Your will.

The Potter and the Clay

> Or does not the potter have a right over the clay, to make from the same lump one vessel for honorable use, and another for common use?
>
> ROMANS 9:21 (NASB)

I love the bumper sticker that says, "If you feel far from God, guess who moved?" So often we tighten the lids on our hearts and put ourselves on the shelf. Maybe we don't even realize we've done it. Today, let's push off the lid and become obedient to Almighty God, the Master Potter.

In pottery, the true beauty of the clay comes out after the firing in the kiln. The extreme heat produces a chemical reaction that causes the pottery to take on qualities it could never have without the fire.

You can cooperate with what God is accomplishing in your life by allowing Him to take those rough spots in your personality or character, and to refine them into something of beauty.

If you keep a journal, write down the pain you're feeling today that caused you to put yourself on the shelf and tighten the lid! Picture yourself pushing off that lid and allowing the Lord to continue healing and reshaping your beautiful vessel. Let Him make you into fine porcelain!

Simple Pleasures

The idea of beauty is simplicity and tranquillity.

—JOHANN WOLFGANG VON GOETHE

Wisdom for Living

Lord, I know I have failed You in so many ways. And yet,
You are always there to receive me unto Yourself. Your love and
Your peace are the dearest things in my life.

Spiritual Renewal Through Simplicity

> *Therefore the redeemed of the Lord shall return, and come with singing unto Zion...they shall obtain gladness and joy; and sorrow and mourning shall flee away.*
>
> ISAIAH 51:11 (KJV)

We all need time to recharge the batteries of our spirits, and time for meaningful moments with our families. One of the reasons I believe in home organization is that it can give us a few extra minutes we need to spend a quiet moment with the Lord or with someone we love. Try these few ideas for added simplicity in your kitchen!

Purchase a large, plastic lazy Susan to store cleaning items under the kitchen sink. I also use them in linen closets, the sewing room, the baby's room, the refrigerator, or under bathroom sinks for shampoos, hair spray, creams, whatever.

If you're having a party and need some extra cooking space, create that space by placing trays or cookie sheets across pulled-out drawers!

Did you know you can sharpen your garbage disposal blades by running ice cubes through them?

The bottom line is to organize your life so that you have time for rest, for spiritual renewal, and for fun with your family.

Simple Pleasures

As for cooking, I mean to begin giving you lessons...
But you're so feather-brained, Anne...You've got to keep
your wits about you in cooking and not stop in the middle...
to let your thoughts rove all over creation.

—LUCY MAUD MONTGOMERY, *ANNE OF GREEN GABLES*

Wisdom for Living

*I need to enter into Your rest today. Every day, Lord,
but especially today. Ease the pounding of my heart
by the quieting of my mind. Amen and amen.*

> *For in the time of trouble he shall hide me in his pavilion: in the secret of his tabernacle shall he hide me; he shall set me up upon a rock.*
>
> PSALM 27:5 (KJV)

The book of Ecclesiastes says, "There is a time for everything and a season for every activity under heaven." Oh, that we would truly take that to heart, and slowly but surely find the time and the season for every activity under heaven. Here are some ideas that can help you start to live that kind of life.

Our bodies have a natural clock. Use your body clock to time activities to your energy level.

Holidays and special occasions are mostly predictable! Shop once a year for birthday and anniversary cards. Then, you'll have what you need when you need it!

Keep a gift shelf in your home for emergencies. As you shop throughout the year, be on the lookout for that special item that could serve a multitude of purposes—housewarming, birthday, get well, or "thank you for your hospitality." Have a gift wrap box or drawer. And remember, it doesn't have to be perfect!

There's a time for everything and a season for every activity. Start today to find it!

Simple Pleasures

* When was the last time you took a bath in the middle of the afternoon?
* Or a shower in the morning *and* evening?
* Or crawled in bed—under the covers—for a nap?

Wisdom for Living

A thousand leaves on a tree and You tell me to pick one.
Lord, I don't know where to begin. Only You can show me the way.
I trust You to guide me, so I'll pick…this one!

Are You There, Lord?

I will never desert you, nor will I ever forsake you.

HEBREWS 13:5 (NASB)

"Are you there, Lord?" This is the question ringing in my mind this morning. With all the things I'm facing, I can't seem to sense that He is near and ready to guide me through the day. Here are a few words from my heart to yours!

There's something about pain that brings us down to the basics of who we are, what we can trust, and what is truly important. When your energy is limited, extraneous matters seem, well, extraneous. There's nothing like suffering to make a person throw out what doesn't work and cling desperately to what proves real and true.

The one reality that stares me in the face whenever I'm hurting the most is how much I need my heavenly Father to be near. First Peter 5:10 calls Him the God of all grace. I am insufficient for the challenges in my life. But He is sufficient.

God is there today, for you and for me. I always knew it. But now I *know* it. And in your own time of testing, if you keep yourself open to His working in your life, you will know it, too.

Simple Pleasures

Read a selection of truly classic Christian literature:

- *The Confessions of St. Augustine*
- *Hinds Feet in High Places*
- *Knowledge of the Holy*
- *My Utmost for His Highest*

Wisdom for Living

Lord, You are my helper, and I know it.
I'll let it make a difference today in all I do.

Flowers Are Spirit Lifters

Yea, the Lord shall give that which is good; and our land shall yield her increase.

PSALM 85:12 (KJV)

There's something about flowers that always lifts my spirits. Maybe it's the delightful colors or the interesting shapes and sizes. I think we love to view anything that is vibrant and alive. Flowers can stir a heart of gratitude in almost every woman I know.

Fresh flowers are such an inexpensive—and simple—way of saying "I cherish my home." You don't need a dozen roses from the florist. A bunch of daisies from the supermarket or an iris from your yard can proclaim, "Love lives here."

Flowers also don't need to be confined to vases. My gifted daughter, Jenny, graced the tops of our bureaus with a beautiful tangle of silk flowers and plants. Be bold; be expressive. Open your heart and allow your teachable spirit to develop a home filled with caring and warmth and growth.

Today, let's be as flowers and allow the joy and peace of our Lord to permeate the walls of our homes and the rooms of our lives with a spirit of loveliness that only Christ Himself can give.

Simple Pleasures

"You'll be using the best tea set, of course, Marilla," she said.
"Can I fix the table with ferns and wild roses?"

— LUCY MAUD MONTGOMERY, *ANNE OF GREEN GABLES*

Wisdom for Living

I see Your gentle touch on my life each day, dear Lord.
You are the Master Gardener, tending to the garden of my soul.
Thank You. The beauty You are creating is a delight!

"Fill My Cup, Lord!"

*My soul longed and even yearned
for the courts of the Lord; My
heart and my flesh sing for joy to
the living God.*

PSALM 84:2 (NASB)

One of my favorite gospel songs is "Fill My Cup, Lord." The message of that song has been dear to my heart for years.

Long before I began my collection of lovely china teacups, years before my first child was born, before I had to work at dieting, before my writing and speaking ministry seemed to be a possibility, something deep in my spirit echoed the cry of that song. Little did I know then how life can truly drain us. Today I know more.

"Fill my cup" remains the constant cry of my thirsty heart. As life matures and we find the responsibilities and pressures mounting, this simple prayer can mean the difference between operating on empty and having a cup that runs over for those we love and serve.

I'm imagining you today with a cup of tea beside you and a quiet moment that you've managed to carve out of our day. Just for a moment, there are no ringing phones or crying children. Come as you are, cup in hand! It's so simple—"Fill my cup, Lord!"

Simple Pleasures

- Pamper your skin with a bar of creamy herbal soap.
- Apply a clarifying facial mask and bask your body in a tub of hot water.
- Give yourself a manicure, or better yet, let a friend do this for you.

Wisdom for Living

*I am empty without You, Lord. Today, I bring my open hands
and my open heart before Your throne. You are the great Giver.
Fill my cup, Lord, that I may pour out Your life on others.*

Child-Friendly, Not Childproof

> *O man, what is good; and what doth the Lord require of thee, but to do justly, and to love mercy, and to walk humbly with thy God?*
>
> MICAH 6:8 (KJV)

It's all a matter of perspective, but I'd like to encourage you to make your home child-friendly today.

There are many children today who feel displaced—literally unwelcome in their own home. Oh how that grieves my heart. We need to establish households where children feel free to be children, where they can be brought up in the nurture and admonition of the Lord, as the Bible says.

A child-friendly house is not just a gift to the children who live there, it's a gift to anyone who visits. It's a sign that this is a house where the whole person is nurtured.

A child-friendly house is a place where you can learn, a place where you can make mistakes and be forgiven. It's a place where you can share, where you can always find something that is just your size in a world that often feels too big.

In God's presence we find this same child-friendly atmosphere for us big kids, too!

Simple Pleasures

- Keep a supply of Popsicles or ice cream sandwiches for young visitors.
- Go on a field trip in your yard—see how many insects you can find.
- Dig earthworms with a flashlight, and then go fishing!

Wisdom for Living

Walking, sitting, standing—whatever I do today, Lord,
may I live and move and have my being in You.

Beauty, Beauty Everywhere

And let not your adornment be external only...but let it be the hidden person of the heart, with the imperishable quality of a gentle and quiet spirit, which is precious in the sight of God.

1 PETER 3:3-4 (NASB)

My constant prayer is this: "Lord, may the love of Christ permeate my heart and life, and spread its gentle fragrance into the lives and hearts of those I meet each day."

With the stresses and strains of everyday living, I've come to realize the importance of rejuvenating my own spirit. We all need spirit lifters—simple things that add beauty and grace to our lives. Try a few of the following ideas and see if you don't feel renewed and ready for a new day.

Next time you take a walk, pick a few flowers. Tuck them in a vase by your bed, on your husband's side. Share beauty with the man in your life.

For your walk or workout, invest in something pretty. If you wear a suit to the office, try the old-fashioned custom of wearing a rosebud or a tiny bunch of violets on your lapel. Add touches of beauty to the everyday aspects of life.

Enjoy a bubble bath by candlelight while sipping iced tea or warm cocoa. Meditate on 1 Peter 3:3-5 as a reminder to cultivate your inner beauty.

Simple Pleasures

The best and most beautiful things in the world cannot be seen or even touched. They must be felt with the heart.

—HELEN KELLER

Wisdom for Living

May Your gentleness and quietness pervade my spirit, O Lord.

Capturing the Spirit of Stillness

He got up, rebuked the wind and said to the waves, "Quiet! Be still!" Then the wind died down and it was completely calm.

I urge you to develop a spirit of stillness in your life. It doesn't have to be difficult. There are simple ways you can provide that quiet, serene place that invites you to stillness.

One of the rooms in my home I love most is my bedroom. When Bob and I moved into our first home, one of our first decisions was to put the television in one of the other rooms. We were committed to developing a room that would be a sanctuary from the world—a place to escape and refill our spirits with God's Word and with love. Your bedroom doesn't need to be just a room where you go to sleep.

Develop an atmosphere of stillness. Give some thought to the lighting, the carpet, the bedclothes, and the fabrics. Let everything create a place of refuge and enjoyment. My nightstand is a small, old oak table with tall legs covered with a cross-stitched white cloth. It holds a Bible, fresh flowers, and an oil lamp.

Spend some effort to make your bedroom a welcoming, restful place.

Simple Pleasures

- Close your eyes and dream of a favorite place from long ago.
- Close your eyes and remember the smell of a mother or grandmother.
- Close your eyes and feel the embrace of a father, a brother, a friend.

Wisdom for Living

Lord, just as You told the waves of the Galilee, "Quiet, be still," calm the waves in my soul. Still the waters; come to me and bring me peace.

Pure and Simple

The Lord protects the simplehearted; when I was in great need, he saved me.

PSALM 116:6

If you want to have a more meaningful quiet time, try this pure and simple advice.

Clutter wearies the spirit! Take at least 15 minutes to "dejunk" the room where you spend your quiet time.

A meaningful quiet time includes food for the soul, so keep your Bible, paper, and a pen on your bedside table, handy for those still moments.

Let this new season of quiet start by reading Ecclesiastes 3. As you read the whole chapter, you will realize that there is a time for every pursuit under heaven. Consider from that chapter what time in life it is for you now. What percentage of your life is available for inward pursuits?

Don't hesitate to take time out for quiet when everything in life gets to be too much. Set a timer for 15 minutes and disappear if you can. If you work outside the home, take a walk somewhere quiet and lovely. Drive to a park. Read, pray, and return to your job refreshed. It's time to make time for quiet time—pure and simple!

Simple Pleasures

- Hand water your flowers instead of turning on the sprinklers.
- Fill your birdbath and keep it full through the hot summer.
- A set of chimes helps to make a cool patio restful and melodic.

Wisdom for Living

It's time to simplify my life, Lord. I know it. I call my soul to rest before You and I ask for the grace to obey what I know You are calling me to do.

> *Let every thing that hath breath praise the Lord. Praise ye the Lord.*
>
> PSALM 150:6 (KJV)

Who hasn't received a lovely card that just begged to be framed and hung on a wall? There are so many ideas that are "suitable for framing!" Here are a few ideas to consider around your home.

Interesting note cards, hats (one of *my* favorites), antique handkerchiefs—all these items make for wonderful framed wall decorations. A favorite verse or prayer beautifully framed says so much when someone visits your home.

If you're a little daring, try hanging up an old window—glass, curtains, and all! Another idea that has worked in our home is to hang tools with interesting shapes or our family's musical instruments in appropriate places.

Here's one I bet you've never thought about: how about hanging a small chair and let it double as a small shelf? And don't forget those old report cards and mementos from your children's school days. They can still be a blessing to your grown children.

What precious memories you can have—right on your wall!

Simple Pleasures

- Open the doors and build a fire in your fireplace on a summer day.
- Play a game of chess or checkers by the fireside.
- Spend an hour in the morning drawing, reading, writing—indulging your pleasures.

Wisdom for Living

I praise You, Lord, for the memories of my life.
I praise You for life and health.

Children of Order

Give thanks to the Lord, for he is good. His love endures forever.

PSALM 136:1

One of the great desires of parents, grandparents, aunts, or uncles is to pass on to their children the strengths and wisdom that God has deposited into their lives. I've been working at this for years with my own children, and I'm happy to report that in the area of organization, both my children, now grown, are more organized than I am. These tips worked for me!

Every Sunday evening, review the family calendar together to make sure everyone is on the same page for the week.

Color-code your children. Yes, I'm serious. Color is something that children understand! Jenny knew yellow towels were hers, and Brad knew his were blue.

Each child needs to understand the importance of keeping a tidy bedroom. Plastic bins and wooden crates can help children organize their things. Make sure each child has a place to hang clothes and store belongings, and a study center for schoolwork with a bulletin board for special items.

You can pass along skills that will make the lives of your children so much easier. I've tried it—it works. Just remember to keep it simple!

Simple Pleasures

- Before you get out of bed, thank God for another day of living.
- Enjoy a tall glass of cold buttermilk, or drink it right out of the carton.
- Toasty muffins, melting butter, and hot coffee are wonderful before the sun rises.

Wisdom for Living

Every wonder of eternal value proceeds from Your heart and hand, dear Lord. Let me be Your servant to bring Your goodness to the world.

The Creative Mother

But when she could hide him no longer, she got a papyrus basket for him and coated it with tar and pitch. Then she placed the child in it and put it among the reeds along the bank of the Nile.

EXODUS 2:3

There may be no more creative mother in Scripture than the mother of Moses! Even today we have to be creative to find solutions to the challenges that confront us. Listen to what one mother told me she finally came to after many frustrating nights with her young daughter.

Nothing I could say or do seemed to work with my five-year-old when it came to staying in bed after we had put her down for the night. After many nights of interrupted sleep, I finally hit on a solution that worked—at least most nights.

I set out two bowls. I labeled one bowl *Mom's Bed Buttons*, and the other *Christine's Bed Buttons*. I put 25 small buttons in each. Every night that Christine goes to bed *and stays in bed*, I owe her one button. She owes me one if she gets up!

The wonderful part is what happens when her button bowl is finally full: we get to do something special—a roller skating trip or some other outing of her choice.

Now she only gets up if she really feels she has to. It was just that simple!

When you find yourself frustrated and a little on edge, take a few moments to explore some creative alternatives. You might be surprised how simple the answer can be. Children are a treasure—so are creative moms.

Simple Pleasures

- Sing to children as they fall asleep.
- Kneel down beside the bed to say prayers.
- Remember a phone call from an aunt or uncle that says, "I'm thinking of you."

Wisdom for Living

Thank You, Lord, for my mother. For all that I remember of her sacrificial parenting and for all she did that I will never know—thank You, Lord.

Love All Around

My soul will be satisfied as with the richest of foods; with singing lips my mouth will praise you.

PSALM 63:5

Think of it—we have the opportunity to fashion our lives and our homes into works of art. What a wonderful goal to create a home—a work of art—that says, "There's love all around."

One way I've discovered to bring love into my home is through what I call our "love shelf." This is a special area in our home where I display those little creative gifts that have come from friends and family over the years. I update it periodically so that there is always something new and interesting to share with others. It's a wonderful way to say, "Your gift means everything to me!"

Surprisingly, a collection is another way to bring love into your home. It's fun and your loved ones will never lack for gift-giving ideas.

Add a creative touch to the everyday. In other words, play! Add a ribbon around your napkins or tuck a fresh flower in some unexpected place. Or simply make yourself a second cup of coffee and take it outside for a moment of fresh air. Create loving moments in the everyday things you do.

Celebrate His love creatively today in your home and in your life.

Simple Pleasures

- Develop the country habit. Fall in love with nature and its surprises.
- Early in the morning, open every window in your house.
- Step out into the early morning garden, cup of coffee in hand.

Wisdom for Living

You are re-creating my life, Jesus. What a hope and promise I have in You! Hallelujah! Give me Your patience as You work in me, even this day.

Creativity Is Sharing

Teach me to do Thy will, For Thou art my God; let Thy good Spirit lead me on level ground.

PSALM 143:10 (NASB)

Did you know that creativity isn't just for self-fulfillment? Much of the joy is in sharing it with others. In fact, the book of Genesis tells us that God created human beings in order to have fellowship. His creative handiwork produced a beautiful garden home for the first man and woman. His heart was to bless them with His creative glory!

We first learned this truth as children, as we crayoned masterpieces for people we loved. The real joy came in running to Mommy and Daddy to share our handiwork. And we still experience the joy of creating and sharing when we cross-stitch a Scripture for a friend, or when we write up a recipe for a new acquaintance.

Once when I was recovering from surgery, a dear friend came to my hospital room with a "recovery kit." In a pretty basket she'd wrapped gifts labeled, Day One, Day Two, and so on. Each day I opened a special gift: a sweet card, a refrigerator magnet, a little puzzle, a can of chicken soup, and even an apple to keep the doctor away!

The simple gift of creativity is really the gift of ourselves.

Simple Pleasures

- Organize a croquet tournament on the back lawn.
- Serve flavored iced tea in colorful tumblers.
- Pause to enjoy adirondack chairs worn to gray by weather's smiles and tears.

Wisdom for Living

I present my life—the minutes, the hours, the days—to You.
Use me for Your eternal purposes and for Your steadfast aims.

A True Lady

But Mary treasured up all these things and pondered them in her heart.

LUKE 2:19

When I was a little girl, I read the famous classic *Little Women* and dreamed of being a lady. Softness and lace, a love of beauty—these images of femininity shaped my earliest ideas of loveliness.

Have we lost that kind of femininity today? I don't believe so. The world has changed, but somewhere in the heart of most of us is a little girl who longs to be a lady. With all the competing images of womanhood and femininity, it's just a little harder to find today. But I believe it's still there.

Being a woman created by God is such a privilege, and the gift of our femininity is something we can give to the people around us. It can be as simple as sharing a moment of beauty, or a gentle touch. Our femininity can express itself in a million simple and gentle ways. It's nothing more than warming up a cold, no-nonsense atmosphere with an aura of caring.

For me, a real lady is a woman with an eye and ear for others, and a heart for God. Isn't that a wonderful definition? It leaves all kinds of room for you to be the woman God intended you to be, and it keeps the focus where it belongs—on the spirit of a woman. Be a lady today!

Simple Pleasures

* Call your father and tell him there's no one like him in the whole world.
* Send a lovely card to your mother—it's always Mother's Day!
* Hug a sibling in person or by phone. Don't let them forget you care.

Wisdom for Living

Father, thank You that I am Your daughter. May my life reflect Your goodness and peace. Let me be a witness to Your greatness today.

July

MENDING FENCES

The Number-One Time Robber

The sluggard craves and gets nothing, but the desires of the diligent are fully satisfied.

PROVERBS 13:4

Failing to plan the day is one of the top time wasters. It goes right along with putting things off or trying to do everything yourself. It's time to get back to the basics. Start today to make it a priority to plan the day, before the day plans you!

Group tasks together like telephone calls, cooking, or letter writing. Schedule blocks of time to get them done.

Here's a big one to work on: promise less, deliver more. Remember, if you can't manage your time, you won't be able to manage any other part of your life.

Meditate on this wonderful paraphrase of Ephesians 5:16: "Time is a daily treasure that attracts many robbers!" There are many things that will steal your time and rob you of the focus you need to follow the Lord in the things He has called you to do. Be aware. You are protecting a valuable treasure.

And today, set aside at least an hour of personal time to replenish your body, your mind, and your soul. Let the Lord give you discipline to break bad habits of neglect and develop new ones of healthy concern and responsibility. You can do it!

Simple Pleasures

- Hum a patriotic song all day long.
- Hang a flag in front of your home. Start the tradition this year.
- Visit a nearby cemetery and reflect on the lives given for freedom.

Wisdom for Living

Teach me to discipline my mind, Father. I am so distracted by all the sights and sounds of this age. I want to set my heart on You today above all else. I delight to sing Your praises.

The Courage of Creativity

Not that we are competent to claim anything for ourselves, but our competence comes from God.

2 CORINTHIANS 3:5

You can be creative in your home and in every area of your life! Sometimes all it takes is courage and remembering to *keep it simple!* God intended life to be an exciting adventure, and if we take Him up on that offer, we will find creativity around every corner.

My husband Bob and I visited some friends who just moved into a tiny mountain cabin full of "inherited" wicker furniture. My friend Irene painted all the old wicker white. Then, buying discounted fabric, she soon had plump, colorful cushions brightening the chairs and sofas. The bedroom wall, and even the bathroom, was "papered" with sheets. For less than a hundred dollars, Irene turned a dingy cabin into a dreamy retreat.

Encouraged by her friends, Irene eventually became an interior designer. A wonderful career and ministry have grown out of Irene's willingness to use her God-given talents to transform what she has been given into a thing of beauty and blessing to herself and others.

Simple Pleasures

- Find a village green on a summer's eve and watch the people pass by.
- Watch a parade from a folding chair with a cold ice tea—take part in the celebration.
- Host an old-fashioned barbecue with hot dogs, potato chips, and watermelon.

Wisdom for Living

I know that You have placed the creative ability within me, Father.
Release Your creativity in me today. May the expressions
of my life reflect Your goodness.

139

How Does Your Garden Grow?

So shall my word be that goeth forth out of my mouth: it shall not return unto me void, but it shall accomplish that which I please, and it shall prosper in the thing whereto I sent it.

ISAIAH 55:11 (KJV)

The little four-year-old was in tears. She couldn't understand why her older brother was mowing down the pretty yellow "flowers" in their overgrown lawn. No amount of explanation would convince her that they weren't flowers, but weeds, and therefore, had to go!

The psalmist said, "As for man [and woman], his days are like grass, he flourishes like a flower of the field." The psalmist admonishes us to live in light of life's brevity. As you look at the garden of your life today, ask yourself, are you growing weeds or flowers? It's all a matter of perspective. Take a few minutes to evaluate your attitudes. They can have a profound effect on how we view the circumstances of our lives.

Are you in need of an attitude adjustment? There's no doubt about it, nothing sets the tone for loveliness and joy like flowers. Even the most ordinary day can become a little more special with flowers. And if you can't afford that expensive bouquet, maybe you can pick a few misplaced "flowers" from your yard or garden to fill a pretty vase in your home or office.

Simple Pleasures

One should lie empty, open, choiceless as a beach—
waiting for a gift from the sea.

—ANNE MORROW LINDBERGH

Wisdom for Living

Teach me to sort through the things that are growing in my life, Lord. Show me what needs to go, and where You plan to do a little pruning.

Neat Is Not Necessarily Organized

Blessed are the pure in heart: for they shall see God.

MATTHEW 5:8 (KJV)

You've heard the old saying, "Cleanliness is next to godliness." Purity in your life comes out of a clean heart. Jesus made that possible with His sacrifice on the cross. Once the inner life has been set right with God, He doesn't stop there. God wants to bring order to every area of our lives. And even though you may be neat, you may not be organized!

Get organized by involving the whole family. Learn to delegate jobs and responsibilities to other members of the family. When something is broken, my Bob is "Mr. Fix-It." Children should receive chores that are age-appropriate. Most importantly, don't do something yourself that another member of the family can do.

My favorite way to get organized is to use a three-ring binder, three-by-five cards, and journals to keep track of all our stuff. Look around to see how other people do things. The important thing is to find out what works for you.

Why bother? Being organized brings some sanity to your world and gives you time for the really important things in your life.

Simple Pleasures

- Put on a warm robe and take a steaming cup of coffee to a wooden deck chair at sunrise.
- Practice the art of solitude.
- While away the afternoon with a good book and a rocking chair.

Wisdom for Living

Help me to move through this day guided by Your Spirit, not pushed to and fro by all my activities. I want my life to be one of peace, not pressure.

Paperwork Slave

If you find yourself buried in paper, take heart—there's hope! But you'll have to learn to *keep it simple!* Being a slave to anything but the love of God will always lead to bondage. Begin your move towards liberation today. Here are six simple steps to free you from the slavery of paperwork:

1. Schedule set times for sorting through papers—a few each day.
2. Get a file cabinet or boxes, plastic trash bags, file folders, and marking pens.
3. Start with whatever room bothers you the most and get rid of the paper!
4. Throw away! Be determined. Make decisions and toss it!
5. File.
6. Store! Store files in a closet, garage, attic, or some other area out of sight, yet accessible. Get rid of some of the clutter so that you have freedom for the important things.

I love the thought in 1 Corinthians 3:13 (NASB) —"each man's [or woman's] work will become evident; for the day will show it…" Take one step. Begin today.

Simple Pleasures

There are other beaches to explore. There are more shells to find. This is only a beginning.

—ANNE MORROW LINDBERGH

Wisdom for Living

Help me today, Lord, to keep my heart and mind focused on You, Your goodness, and Your blessing in my life.

Be Content in Everything

> The Lord is my portion, saith my soul; therefore will I hope in him. The Lord is good unto them that wait for him, to the soul that seeketh him.
>
> LAMENTATIONS 3:24-25 (KJV)

One of the Barnes' famous sayings is "If you're not happy with what you have, you'll never be satisfied with what you want!" I challenge you today to learn to be content in everything!

I meet so many people who are always looking to the next paycheck, the next home, the next month. When we find ourselves looking to the future because we aren't content with today, life can get pretty complicated.

Let me give you a few simple thoughts for reflection. Hopefully they will lead you to act and to find greater contentment.

Instead of being *preoccupied* with your situation in life, start *praising* God for where you are.

Ask God to reveal to you what you are to learn in your present situation, regardless of the circumstances.

Finally, write a letter to God thanking Him for all your blessings— name them individually! A grateful heart is the first step to true contentment.

Simple Pleasures

- Lilacs are the essence of pleasure. Plant a lilac bush in your garden.
- Capture a firefly.
- Wicker chairs and plump pillows invite a moment's pause.

Wisdom for Living

Lord, I wait on You to reveal Your will in the situation facing me. I trust You, and I know that You have promised that all things work together for good to those who love You and are the called according to Your purpose.

One Day at a Time

It is good that a man should both hope and quietly wait for the salvation of the Lord.

LAMENTATIONS 3:26 (KJV)

So many of us are overwhelmed by the pressures and responsibilities we face—yet we keep taking on more. We haven't learned to say no! Let's get off that treadmill and make life simpler!

Today, begin to live one day at a time. Go to the Lord each day and seek His guidance and wisdom—just for today!

Take a pad of paper and list only those things that need to be done today. After a few days, you'll find yourself having to rank your activities by priority, certain things being more important than others. As your To Do list becomes more complex, concentrate on the most important activity first and let the least important items settle to the end of the day.

At night, as you crawl into bed, look at your list, smile, and thank God for helping you stay on schedule. Thank Him for giving you the power to say no.

Finally, thank Him for the things that you didn't get done. Life is dynamic, and it will continue to be so as long as we live. It won't be finished until it's finished.

Simple Pleasures

- Develop a passion for living properly—simply.
- Write a letter by oil lamplight or candlelight.
- Go barefoot all day.

Wisdom for Living

Father, teach me to wait for Your timing alone.
Teach me to move by Your Spirit and to trust You for the outcome.

Coming Forth as Gold

O Lord, thou hast pleaded the causes of my soul; thou hast redeemed my life.

LAMENTATIONS 3:58 (KJV)

Everyone has experienced some kind of tragedy. The important thing is the way that we handle these events when they happen.

I grew up with a violent, alcoholic father. I had no place to go and no one to talk to, so I pushed my pain down the best I could and carried on. Today, there are many wonderful support groups for people in pain. Many of these groups can be found in local churches. There's no need to be in a desperate situation alone.

Job 23:10 says, "But he knows the way that I take; when he has tested me, I will come forth as gold."

What a promise to hold on to! What a comfort to know that He not only knows the path laid out for me, but that He is somehow involved in the testing in a way that will be for my good.

Whatever your test is today, don't go through the testing alone. Jesus knows and understands your pain. He is always with us to help us get through the tough times. Simply trust Him. Like Job, you too will "come forth as gold."

Simple Pleasures

* Invest in a set of fine knives.
* Splurge on a new cookbook, one that features Italian or Mexican fare.
* Drizzle garlic with oil and roast in the oven. The smell is heavenly.

Wisdom for Living

Jesus, You are the great Redeemer. Thank You for taking every aspect of my life and molding it and shaping it to look like You.

The Art of Creative Seeing

While we look not at the things which are seen, but at the things which are not seen: for the things which are seen are temporal; but the things which are not seen are eternal.

2 CORINTHIANS 4:18 (KJV)

Consider this: some of what can keep life simple for us and those we love is what I call *the art of creative seeing.*

In Ephesians 1:18 (NASB), Paul says, "I pray that the eyes of your heart may be enlightened, so that you will know what is the hope of His calling." How's that for creative seeing? But can it be applied on a practical level as well? I believe it can.

So much of the time, all we need is the hope to look beyond what appear to be the limitations of our abilities and resources. All it takes is a bit of ingenuity to discover wonderful possibilities in every area of our lives.

Start with your familiar old possessions. Any old piece of furniture can be painted, refinished, or covered—and very inexpensively. A crystal salt shaker can hold a miniature bouquet on a nightstand.

Need to get more exercise? Take a nearby friend some flowers and enjoy the fresh air at the same time. Looking for time alone with God? It can happen while you wash the dishes. Practice the art of creative seeing.

Simple Pleasures

- Peas or beans eaten right off the vine are one of summer's wonders.
- Gathering fresh eggs can be an adventuresome morning ritual.
- Learn to brew espresso and enjoy the aroma of fresh ground coffee.

Wisdom for Living

Lord, You've called me! What could be better than that? Help me to understand that calling. It's from You, it's personal, and it's for me!

Breaking the Rules

If we are out of our mind, it is for the sake of God; if we are in our right mind, it is for you. For Christ's love compels us...

2 CORINTHIANS 5:13-14

As women, we oftentimes want things to be "just right" around our homes. We love to decorate and create a lovely environment for our families and friends to come to. But we must always keep in mind that a beautifully decorated house still has to function as a home.

Strive for a home that is truly welcoming to the people who live there. Decorate for your family first. Your husband shouldn't have to perch in chairs that feel too small. He should be able to recline in one that feels like "home" to him. Your children shouldn't have to avoid certain rooms. They can learn to play within reasonable limitations, but they need to feel like your home is also theirs.

Don't fool yourself about how your family lives! If your husband watches TV a lot, don't hide the set under a side table. If your children are more studious types, then find a way to give them a space where they can comfortably do their work.

And don't forget Psalm 127:1 (NASB): "Unless the LORD builds the house, they labor in vain who build it." That puts it all in perspective, doesn't it?

Simple Pleasures

- Push back the furniture and have a family slumber party.
- Plan a family game night and have lots of goodies.
- Turn out the lights, build a fire in the fireplace, and roast marshmallows.

Wisdom for Living

Dear Lord, I want to be compelled by Your Spirit. Show me my true calling. If You don't build my house, I don't want it built.

147

Count Your Blessings

Let the word of Christ dwell in you richly as you teach and admonish one another with all wisdom.

COLOSSIANS 3:16

When was the last time you stopped for a moment, just to count your blessings?

In Sunday school and church, we've all sung the well-known song, "Count Your Blessings, Name Them One by One." But did you realize that this exercise is good for your mental and physical health as well as your spiritual well-being? Start by asking yourself these questions:

Is anyone a little happier because you came along today? Did you leave someone with any concrete evidence of your kindness—any sign of your love? Have you learned something new about life, living, or love?

Have you gone through the day without worrying over what you don't have, and celebrating the things you do have? Did you try to think of someone in a more positive light?

Did you make someone smile or laugh today? Have you forgiven others for being less than perfect? Have you attempted to mend a torn relationship?

It's a simple formula—just "count your blessings"!

Simple Pleasures

Spend all you have for loveliness,
Buy it and never count the cost;
For one white singing hour of peace,
Count many a year of strife well-lost.
And for a breath of ecstasy,
Give all you have been, or could be.

—SARA TEASDALE, "BARTER"

Wisdom for Living

Thank You, Lord, for the simplest thing I can think of right now—thank You for love. Everything I have, everything I am is from Your hand.

A Good Night's Sleep

I will lie down and sleep in peace, for you alone, O Lord, make me dwell in safety.

PSALM 4:8

Some say we are a sleep-deprived nation. When was the last time *you* had a good night's rest? Here are some tips that have been passed along to me over the years.

Get up at the same time every morning. It helps your biological clock stay in sync. Get a minimum of 30 minutes of strenuous exercise a day.

Don't go to bed too hungry or too full. Limit drinking all liquids a few hours before bedtime. Cut back on caffeine—it's a powerful stimulant. Nicotine is an even stronger stimulant than caffeine.

Set aside time to unwind. Keep your bedroom from becoming another office or TV room. Before you go to bed, read a favorite devotional, listen to some music, meditate, and pray.

Matthew 11:28 quotes Jesus as saying, "Come to me...I will give you rest!" You can't be at your best if you are tired day in and day out. We shortchange ourselves and those we love if we live tired lives.

Simple Pleasures

Make haste, slowly.

—CAESAR AUGUSTUS

Wisdom for Living

Rest. O Lord, I need it badly. Help me to realize again that true rest is found in You; not in sleep, or vacation, or a moment's peace and quiet. Rest is from Your hand alone. I come to You, Lord.

Healthy Bodies

Do not be wise in your own eyes; fear the Lord and shun evil. This will bring health to your body and nourishment to your bones.

PROVERBS 3:7-8

Our body is one of God's most precious gifts to us, believe it or not! Each of us has the responsibility to understand how her body works and to work to take care of it. If you have been a little lax lately, I hope these tips help in getting you back on track.

Always select single-serving sizes of snacks and desserts to help prevent yourself from eating too-large portions. Refrain from talking while you eat—it's all too easy to down a lot of food without realizing it. At parties, survey the buffet and decide on two or three items—maximum.

Always remove the skin from poultry. You'll automatically reduce calories by about 25 percent. Put your salad dressing in a small spray bottle and mist your salads. You'll get the taste without a lot of the calories.

Substitute club soda for your daily regular soda and shed one pound per month. Get active—always take the stairs, and walk if you don't have to drive.

Good health just makes sense!

Simple Pleasures

The good and the wise lead quiet lives.

—EURIPIDES

Wisdom for Living

*Dear Father, please help me to discipline myself to exercise.
Help me to say no to one more serving of dessert.
I'm encouraged that You will help today!*

A Way of Life

Enter into his gates with thanksgiving, and into his courts with praise: be thankful unto him, and bless his name.

PSALM 100:4 (KJV)

When you're grateful for your place in God's family, *welcome* becomes a way of life. You'll find that your heart's desire is to open your life more and more to others instead of shutting them out. And a good place to start is your home. Make your home a place of welcome!

There are a lot of ways to do that—what I like to call...*spirit lifters*. For example, what's the first thing you see when you walk through your front or back door? At the very least, make sure that the entry area is clean and beckoning. First impressions do make a difference!

Does your telephone voice speak a welcome? Is it warm and gracious? The same thing goes for your answering machine. People can tell a lot about you by what they hear in your voice.

Fresh flowers are such an inexpensive way of saying welcome. A bouquet of daisies from the supermarket, an iris from your yard proclaims, "Love lives here! We appreciate the simple, beautiful things of life."

Begin today to ask the Lord to open your life to others. You'll be surprised at how simple it can be to add a welcome to your home—and to your life.

Simple Pleasures

* Restore the tradition of a lovely, chiming, grandfather clock.
* Invite a friend over to enjoy a cozy fire and an evening of quiet reading.
* Gather a group of friends and read poetry aloud at a local park.

Wisdom for Living

Let me roll out the welcome, Lord, to those I love today. Let my life speak of Your goodness and truth. Guide and direct me in all I do and say today.

Forgiveness Keeps Life Clean

How much more shall the blood of Christ, who through the eternal Spirit offered himself without spot to God, purge your conscience from dead works to serve the living God?

HEBREWS 9:14 (KJV)

One morning, as Bob and I were lingering over our coffee, he reached over and pulled a slip of paper from the decorated jar that we always keep on the kitchen table. Long ago, we decided to create this "conversation jar" as a way of keeping our interactions fun and meaningful. In it we placed little slips of paper, each one containing a stimulating discussion question.

This particular morning, Bob selected one that would start me on a long road toward forgiveness. As he read the question, something exploded in me, "What would you do if you could spend one day with your dad?"

It was a loaded question for me because my dad was a desperate alcoholic. Living in our home meant always living on edge, never knowing when he might fly into a rage. I realized that I'd never really forgiven him.

That very day, I began the process of letting God restore my relationship with my father—even though my father was dead. It was hard work! But through the process, the Lord washed me clean—He filled my cup with sparkling forgiveness!

Simple Pleasures

Laugh and the world laughs with you. Cry and you cry alone.

—PROVERB

Wisdom for Living

I know I need to forgive him. I know I haven't quite forgiven her. Jesus, I humble myself before You, knowing that I deserve death and You have offered me forgiveness. Grace me to offer it now to others.

What a Friend

For the earth is the Lord's, and the fulness thereof.

1 CORINTHIANS 10:26 (KJV)

This morning let's grab a cup of coffee, throw the comforter around us, and talk for a minute—you and me! There's nothing like curling up by an old friend and talking to our hearts' content.

Over the years, I've learned that Jesus is the One I can always talk to—the One whose love truly changes my life. I know I can tell Him anything. He always comforts me and loves me. The old hymn really has it right: "What a Friend We Have in Jesus!"

That's what a real friend is, isn't it? A friend can love you in spite of who you are. A friend can fill your life with sharing and closeness and love—with communion.

This kind of friendship is not an easy thing to find in our busy, bustling world. Friendship like this takes time and work. It's a privilege that means thinking of someone else more than yourself and learning what it means to love others as Jesus loves us. No, I won't always get it right. As long as I live in this "broken vessel," my cup will leak!

So that's when I pray, "Oh, fill my cup, Lord. Fill it—with You!"

Simple Pleasures

- Nourish your mind on good literature.
- Keep a reading journal.
- Read psalms aloud. Nurture your soul by the sound of your voice.

Wisdom for Living

Lord, You are my Friend. I want to pour out my heart to You today—all my joys, my sorrows, my expectations…a heart full of thanksgiving.

Charming Chores

Do not conform any longer to the pattern of this world, but be transformed by the renewing of your mind. Then you will be able to test and approve what God's will is—his good, pleasing and perfect will.

Maybe we need to do a simple attitude adjustment about something we all face around the home—chores! They can seem so overwhelming at times, and so *everyday!* Here are some ideas to help keep the joy in this part of our home life.

One thing that has really made a difference for our family is what we call the message center. It isn't elaborate and can be placed anywhere in your home that is convenient and comfortable for every member of the family. You can set it up on the refrigerator, a kitchen bulletin board, or even a family room door.

This is the place where the lives of your family members converge in one place so that everyone is informed and feels a part of the day's and week's activities—and chores!

Encourage everyone to use the message center to list plans, needs for the next shopping trip, and especially important, all telephone messages. Keep it current. Throw away all those outdated notes. Most importantly, simplify and unclutter your life by communicating with each other so everyone is on board with the plan.

Make a commitment today to organize your home with a message center.

Simple Pleasures

* Envision an errand-free weekend. Do it!
* Start a ten-minute exercise routine. Expand it to 20 minutes next week.
* Buy yourself a good hair brush.

Wisdom for Living

Thank You for chores. For the ordinary things of daily living.
I am alive, Lord, and these are the blessings of life.
Help me to find joy in the simple and the ordinary.

Rules You Should Break

So then, those who suffer according to God's will should commit themselves to their faithful Creator and continue to do good.

1 PETER 4:19

There are certain rules that we all know can't be broken without dire consequences. However, when it comes to decorating your house, most of those rules just don't exist. Here are some rules just *made* to be broken!

Rule one: It all has to match. Who said so? Mix your styles, colors, and design periods. It can be visually exciting and surprisingly pleasing. The only guideline might be to have at least one common element, such as a color or design motif, to tie everything together.

Rule two: You need a round cloth for a round table. Draped beautifully, or even tied up at the corners, a square or rectangular cloth does just fine!

Rule three: The sofa goes up against the wall! (Sounds like our mother's house, doesn't it?) Not always! Instead of lining up furniture square against the wall, try an angle or several small conversation groups. Your room will look far more interesting.

One more rule: Keep it simple! Seek out opportunities in each day to rest, plan, regroup, and draw closer to God. That's a rule you don't want to break!

Simple Pleasures

- Unwind with an old movie and a large bowl of popcorn.
- Make Mexican hot chocolate by using Mexican chocolate.
- Scent your home with baking bread or apple pie.

Wisdom for Living

Father, I want my life to be about love, not law; about righteousness, not rules. Show me this day what it means to respond to the life of Your Spirit within me.

"Destuffing" and Other Simple Tasks

You are to bring into the ark two of all living creatures, male and female, to keep them alive with you.

GENESIS 6:19

For most of us our decorating problems can be put under one heading: *stuff!*

It fills our lives and our homes. We don't know where to put it, and we don't know how to use it. Here are some ideas for the stuff in your life!

Screen it! That's right, put a beautiful decorated screen around that unsightly exercise machine. You can paint your screen, texture it, or do whatever you like to make it attractive.

Box it! A set of matching boxes is a great way to stash awkward items. If boxes looks good, keep them right out in the open. If they are more utilitarian, stack them neatly in your attic or spare bedroom.

Make it cute! You can tuck small "stuff" into open baskets or in matched jars, and all of a sudden the stuff looks like it belongs.

Your last option, of course, is to get rid of it! When an item has served its purpose, give it away or get rid of it.

Thank God today for the precious simple things in your life!

Simple Pleasures

* Plan a garage sale and donate the proceeds to charity.
* Purchase a fountain pen or handsome ballpoint. Let it be part of your creative expression, an extension of your personality.
* A clean, organized car is the same as a clean, organized life.

Wisdom for Living

Father, I need to have more of You and fewer things in my life. Guide me this day as I seek to honor You in all I do.

More Management of Stuff

Who can discern his errors? Forgive my hidden faults.

PSALM 19:12

We all have "stuff." It's almost part of being American. But where do you store your stuff? Have fun by thinking creatively about organizing and storing your possessions. The possibilities are limited only by your creativity.

One of my favorite pieces of furniture is an odd little cabinet I bought for $15 at somebody's house many years ago. It's long and low, with doors in front. We use it as a table behind our sofa, with a little lamp and an antique scale on top—but it also offers wonderful storage space.

Whenever I visit an antique store or a secondhand shop, I'm on the lookout for these kinds of multipurpose pieces. If you have an empty corner in a guest room or garage, something simple like this will definitely fit the bill.

Even a simple cardboard box can be one of your best organizational tools. Rescue them from the recycling bin and put them to work in the interest of an organized and attractive work space. With just a little thought and creativity, you can definitely keep everything in its place!

Simple Pleasures

- Enjoy a lunch of a platter of different types of cheese, sliced fruit, and French bread.
- Place an anonymous bouquet of flowers on a neighbor's doorstep.
- Isn't getting snapshots back from the processor fun?

Wisdom for Living

Father, I want Your peace and Your quiet in my life and in my home. I wait on You, dear Lord, to lead me into a new season of simplicity.

Lord, I Need You

Be not ye therefore like unto them: for your Father knoweth what things ye have need of, before ye ask him.

MATTHEW 6:8 (KJV)

Dear friend, you don't have to make an appointment to ask God for something you need, or to thank Him for something you have received. He's interested in everything that happens to you. It's true.

I once heard it said that "prayer is talking with God and telling Him you love Him. It's conversing with God about all the things that are important in life, both large and small, and then being assured that He is listening."

Isn't that a wonderful thought to bring to a busy day? It's so easy to succumb to the pressures and obligations of the day and lose track of how much our Lord cares for all that is happening to us and in us.

As you pause to send your prayer heavenward, maybe He'll bless you with an idea of how you can bless someone you love. How about preparing a "love basket."

Fill it with food for dinner, a surprise lunch, or special items like a candle, fresh flowers, or some tea bags. Use your imagination and creativity. Maybe someone needs you today to say, "I love you."

Simple Pleasures

Courage is the price life extracts for granting peace.

— AMELIA EARHART

Wisdom for Living

Lord, as I cast my cares on You, give me strength to reach out to those who might need my care this day. Amen.

A Bearer of Light

I am the light of the world. Whoever follows me will never walk in darkness, but will have the light of life.

JOHN 8:12

Whether you're great or small in God's kingdom, you are still God's child! Here are some simple reflections from God's heart to yours.

Harriett Buell wrote the words for "A Child of the King" one Sunday morning while walking home from her church service. She sent her text to a Christian magazine and it was printed in the February 1, 1877 issue.

Sometime later a singer and music teacher named John Sumner saw the inspired words and composed the music he felt would best fit the heart of what Harriett Buell was trying to communicate.

The hymn has been widely used since then to remind believers who they really are—bearers of God's image and children of the King of kings.

Romans 8:16 (NASB) tells us, "The Spirit Himself bears witness with our spirit that we are children of God." Have you ever considered that there are two ways of spreading light? You can either be the candle—or the mirror that reflects it. Ms. Buell's light shone forth and John Sumner picked up the reflection. What a joy to spread His light!

Simple Pleasures

When love and skill work together, expect a masterpiece.

—RUSKIN

Wisdom for Living

Your light lights my life, dear Jesus. I pray that its reflection in me will warm those around me and show them more clearly just who You are.

August

THE DEEPER HARVEST

The Teachable Heart

Instruct a wise man and he will be wiser still; teach a righteous man and he will add to his learning.

PROVERBS 9:9

Oh, how I pray for this important quality of character—a teachable heart. Since none of us is perfect to be sure, and life is filled with learning and growing day by day, having a teachable heart is the key to becoming all that God intended us to become.

A woman with a teachable heart is a priceless treasure. She has a heart that can give and forgive, protect and respect! Hers is a heart submitted to God above all. This is the woman that Proverbs says is "worth far more than rubies."

My daughter once gave me a beautiful, fragrant heart sachet as a gift. God was teaching me important lessons at the time about my fragrance before Him and others. That beautiful sachet always reminds me of the sweet fragrance of the Lord Jesus Himself. It also reminds me that I'm called to be a woman after God's own heart.

I pray that His love might permeate your heart today in such a way that you will spread His fragrance to those around you. As surely as night follows day, a teachable heart produces the fragrance of His peace, His love, and His joy.

Simple Pleasures

- Listen to the sound of rain on the roof, especially when you're under the covers.
- Be excited about tomorrow.
- Don't you enjoy finding that you have the exact change you need?

Wisdom for Living

Sometimes my heart wants to harden in bitterness and disappointment.
Soften me by Your love today, Lord, so that I might extend hope
and forgiveness to those You love.

True Riches

Where your treasure is, there your heart will be also.

How true is the age-old adage that "you can't have it all." Since our resources are limited, we must decide how to use the gifts that God has deposited into our lives. I learned a long time ago that people are more important than things. So wisdom suggests we will receive huge dividends if we invest ourselves, our time, and our money in people we love rather than on things that may have no eternal value.

Good money management is important. Luke 16:11 says, "If you have not been trustworthy in handling worldly wealth, who will trust you with true riches?" That's pretty straightforward, isn't it? But don't limit your thinking to just money and gifts. Say no to good things—and save your yes for the best!

Management of our resources is more of an attitude toward the use of our gifts than a systematic plan. Scripture tells us that our "firstfruits" belong to God. Today, purpose to give of the best you have to things that will count for eternity. Invest yourself, your time, and your money in your relationship with the living God and in the lives of others.

Simple Pleasures

- Collect change in jars and someday pass them on to grandchildren.
- Add a touch of lavender to cakes, cookies, and desserts.
- Read day-old newspapers, comforted by the fact that the news is over.

Wisdom for Living

I place the true riches of my life in Your hands today,
O God, and ask You to order my priorities from a heavenly perspective.
All my "firstfruits" I give to You.

Diligence in Simple Things

He also that is slothful in his work is brother to him that is a great waster.

Proverbs 18:9 (KJV)

It's the little things that drive us crazy sometimes. Paying attention to those moments when our frustrations rise up and threaten to undo us can pay important dividends in peace and tranquillity around our homes.

Today, look for simple ways to solve potentially annoying moments.

Are you frustrated every time you store your leftovers after meals, looking for the right lid to fit the right size container? Try marking your bowls and covers with the same number and all you'll have to do is match the numbers.

Or how about those rubber gloves that go on—but you can never get them off because you forgot to sprinkle the insides with powder? Just hold your gloved hands under cold tap water. They slip right off.

To keep bugs out of your flour canister, put a stick of spearmint gum in the flour. It works!

Every single day is made up of many incidental moments. Keeping it simple will give you leftovers for the more important things in life!

Simple Pleasures

She couldn't pass a fern or a berry without wanting to know its pedigree and insisted on getting the Latin name.

—Humphrey Bogart of Katharine Hepburn

Wisdom for Living

Father, teach me today the value of little things. Teach me good stewardship in the little things so that You can entrust me with more.

From a Child's Perspective

The heart of the righteous weighs its answers, but the mouth of the wicked gushes evil.

PROVERBS 15:28

Listen to what some junior high kids said were ways to "get along with your child." These tips can certainly apply to all our relationships!

"Spend time with me, alone, once a week."

"Even though my problems may seem ridiculous to you at times, don't tell me to forget them."

"Lighten up a little. Remember, I'm trying hard to please you."

"Count to ten—or 20—before you confront me!"

"Admit when you're wrong."

"Be honest."

What is it that they say—out of the mouths of babes? Children are our most precious treasure. They not only learn from us, but we can learn from them. Proverbs 22:6 (NASB) holds a wonderful promise: "Train up a child in the way he should go, even when he is old he will not depart from it."

Simple Pleasures

- Rent a paddle boat or canoe and sail the seas near home.
- Fill a glass shaker with powdered sugar—sprinkle on hot French toast.
- Set a table out under a garden tree and serve frosty lemonade.

Wisdom for Living

I struggle to be patient, Lord, and honest. Teach me the glory of Your truth. Slow me down, Lord. Show me how to take time for those around me who need Your love.

Memories to Last a Lifetime

Children's children are the crown of old men; and the glory of children are their fathers.

PROVERBS 17:6 (KJV)

In our busy world it is often difficult to slow down and create for young people the kind of moments that we cherish in our own childhood memories. Just as the Lord Jesus always has time for you, take a few extra moments with a little person you love.

At bedtime, tell your grandchildren the beginning of a dream and suggest that they listen with their eyes closed. Before you know it, they will be sound asleep!

Do a project with your children to emphasize how important our treasures can be and to teach them how to protect them. Take a favorite book and cover the front and each page with clear contact paper. It's a simple way to preserve a future heirloom for your children.

Decorate your children's rooms by having them draw pictures of their favorite activities on butcher paper. Then praise them for their handiwork and hang it on the walls around the room.

Read Bible stories to your children and pray with them. It's an important part of their spiritual heritage, one filled with moments they will treasure for a lifetime.

Simple Pleasures

The days may come, the days may go,
But still the hands of memory weave
The blissful dreams of long ago.

—HENRY TUCKER, "SWEET GENEVIEVE"

Wisdom for Living

O God, I love the heritage I have in You. The prophets of old told of Your righteousness and holiness. That heritage of faith belongs to me. Hallelujah!

A Heritage of Gardening

How precious also are thy thoughts unto me, O God! how great is the sum of them!

PSALM 139:17 (KJV)

Simple things are often the very tools our heavenly Father uses to instruct us, to comfort us, "to train us up in the way we should go." In the same way, the simple things God gives us can bind us to each other.

My grandchildren love to garden. Their little hands till the soil, scatter and cover the seeds, and help with the first watering. What child doesn't love to dig in the dirt? Gardening has become a bonding experience for these children with their Papa as well. As they work with him in the garden, learning responsibility and discovering God's creation, we take every opportunity to reveal how God loves and provides for us. Each time they visit they can't get out of the van fast enough to see how the plants are growing. And you know what? It takes hold of their hearts.

One of my favorite verses of Scripture says, "These words...shall be on your heart. You shall teach them diligently to your sons [and daughters] and shall talk of them when you sit in your house and when you walk by the way" (Deuteronomy 6:6-7 NASB). Profound truth, and yet, oh so simple.

Simple Pleasures

- Search secondhand shops for old gardening books. Start a collection.
- Hang sheets outdoors to catch the summer air. *Nothing* smells better.
- Combine strawberries and grapes with blueberries, raspberries, or peaches—add a mint sprig.

Wisdom for Living

Lord, let me be an example today in all I do and say. May those around me lift their hearts to You because of what they see in my life. Amen.

Life Is "Process"

> And God gave Solomon wisdom and understanding exceeding much, and largeness of heart, even as the sand that is on the sea shore.
>
> 1 KINGS 4:29 (KJV)

I've heard it said that life is five percent joy, five percent grief, and 90 percent maintenance. Are you nodding your head in agreement? Well, if that's the case, we need to find simple ways to make the dailyness of our maintenance program shine with the beauty of God's goodness and joy. How is that possible? I believe it's by finding simple ways to bring loveliness to even the most mundane task!

It's this act of making beauty out of something ordinary that brings joy to our spirits and to the people around us. It may take an attitude adjustment to find delight in serving brunch on miscellaneous, imperfectly matched pottery and linens, but when you share the story of finding the plates at a garage sale, the cups at a local discount store, the tablecloth on a clearance table at J.C. Penney's, and the napkins in the back of your linen closet, you communicate the message that life is *process,* and half the fun is getting there.

Share the spirit of creativity! Your inspiration will cause others to use their God-given creativity to instill a spirit of loveliness into their own lives and homes!

Simple Pleasures

* Garnish desserts with delectable, edible pansies.
* Bundle sprigs of lavender and tie with raffia.
* Play the dictionary game or learn a new word everyday.

Wisdom for Living

Sometimes I feel so small, Lord, so pitiful. Enlarge my heart so that I may be a vessel of blessing to others.

An Eternal Rhythm

But they that wait upon the Lord shall renew their strength; they shall mount up with wings as eagles; they shall run, and not be weary; and they shall walk, and not faint.

ISAIAH 40:31 (KJV)

Over the years, gardening has taught me a lot about who I am as a woman of God. That's right—gardening! It's simple, really.

Through many hours of tilling, planting, weeding, and pruning, I've learned to slow down and smell the roses. The garden forces me to go at God's pace, taking time from a busy schedule of writing and speaking to do the simple daily chores that lead to loveliness. It's an eternal rhythm: sometimes I work, sometimes I wait. Then God does the growing, and I enjoy the results.

I love the fact that God placed the first man and woman in a beautiful garden. Wouldn't you love to have visited that first garden God created? He intended us to be surrounded by beauty from the very beginning. The Psalmist captured the Creator's love for His creature and His creation: "He maketh me to lie down in green pastures. He leadeth me beside the still waters. He restoreth my soul."

Today, place a plant or flower nearby to remind yourself that the beauty of God's handiwork began in a garden, and it continues today in your life.

Simple Pleasures

* Start a list of interests you would like to pursue and keep adding to it.
* Cherish moments of leisure when you have the right to do whatever you want.
* Make a travel list. Think of beautiful places on God's earth you'd still like to see.

Wisdom for Living

Father, I feel so weak today. I need Your touch on my life. Heal me where I hurt inside, dear Lord. I will praise You all the day long.

Treasure Life

In holiness and godly sincerity…in the grace of God, we have conducted ourselves in the world, and especially toward you.

2 CORINTHIANS 1:12 (NASB)

When life seems glum, or things aren't quite going your way, try just keeping it simple—simply treasure life!

Not long ago, my daughter Jenny shared with me something about her growing up years that really meant a lot to her. She said, "Mom, I always heard you and Dad say how blessed and thankful you were for where you were in life. But Mom, I know now that things weren't always that great! Yet you've both never stopped talking about how good God is and how well God provides. I've decided that from now on, I'm going to set a better example in my own home and with my children by saying more often just how blessed and thankful we are. Thanks, Mom, for showing me how to have more gratitude."

What a joy to receive such words from my daughter. When we feel grateful, it affects our whole being. All the trivial issues seem to fall away. Do something today that reflects your love for your treasured life. Discover the joy of simply living life abundantly!

Simple Pleasures

- Think of someone who needs cheering, and do your part.
- Offer overnight babysitting for a young couple that needs a break.
- Invite a neighbor for tea and exchange a lifetime highlight.

Wisdom for Living

I'm alive! Thank You, Lord, for life. Thank You for my life.
I want to celebrate You all day long.

You Can Be a Star

For I know the thoughts that I think toward you, saith the Lord, thoughts of peace, and not of evil, to give you an expected end.

JEREMIAH 29:11 (KJV)

Have you ever thought that you're a star people can touch? Does your life light up the room when you enter? Do your children or your grandchildren reflect back the love you give them? Do you brighten the office and the lives of your coworkers each morning as you start the day?

Each one of us has to start with a new 24 hours every day. Each one of us has seven days in every week. What are you doing with your days and hours?

What are your deepest dreams? Writing a song? Starting a business? Authoring a book? Creating a new recipe? Your life is a star. Don't let that star fall to the ground. As you begin each day, plan to nurture and water your dreams until the Sonlight makes them grow.

Someone once said, "Make big plans. Aim high in hope and work." The Bible says, "Press on toward the goal for the prize of the upward call of God in Christ Jesus" (Philippians 3:14 NASB). And then remember to be on the lookout for those other stars around you! Your encouragement can make a difference for their dreams, too!

Simple Pleasures

- Plant a tree and spend a lifetime watching it grow.
- Press summer flowers to use on cards or special gift wrap.
- Sleep with your windows open—awaken to the morning breeze.

Wisdom for Living

You have a plan for me. A plan that comes out of the heart of a loving God. Thank You, Father, that I am Your child. I know it is Your pleasure to give good gifts to Your children!

If I could only give you one piece of counsel for life, it would be this: simply walk in the steps of Jesus. First Peter 2:21 says, "To this you were called, because Christ suffered for you, leaving you an example, that you should follow in his steps."

There's no doubt, we're fallible human beings. We can't *be* Jesus, of course. But if we develop a teachable spirit, the Lord Jesus Himself can show us the way to life and godliness.

Jesus left us with His example of a godly life. If you can love Him and desire Him with all your soul, mind, and strength, your character will then reveal the likeness of Jesus. Did you know that you become like the ones you love? It's true. Whatever you set your heart upon, that object or person will exercise great influence on your life and character.

As you seek to be like Jesus, you will find yourself reaching out to the helpless, praying for the sick, supporting those in need, and becoming involved in the work of the gospel. As the Lord lives in you, He will form you into the beautiful, marvelous image of God, according to your own uniqueness.

Simple Pleasures

No act of kindness is ever wasted.

—AESOP

Wisdom for Living

I love Your voice, Lord. I listen for it in the morning, throughout the day, and at evening. I hear Your voice and know I belong to You.

The Older Woman

Above all else, guard your heart, for it is the wellspring of life. Put away perversity from your mouth; keep corrupt talk far from your lips.

Not one of us really cherishes the idea of growing older. Watching our children leave home, seeing our own body change into something quite different from what it used to be, and then discovering that one by one, beloved friends and family are slipping into eternity. When I was younger, I always cringed when I read the verse in Titus 2:4, "Then they can train the younger women to love their husbands and children." I thought, I will never be an older woman!

Today I consider it a privilege to be an older woman. I have come to realize how precious it is to have lived life, to have gained some perspectives that enable me to share life truths with other women my age and younger.

One of the most important truths I've found is this: you can never change another person. But God can. I've also discovered that the change usually begins with me. When I begin to change, the other person begins to change.

Be an "older woman" to someone this week. Encourage them to love. Encourage them to pray. Nurture a teachable spirit—in you!

Simple Pleasures

* Buy a simple linen tablecloth and decorate it as the mood dictates.
* Gather on the patio or porch and tell family stories.
* The gift of gladness ages well.

Wisdom for Living

What a privilege to grow old—to live life to the full.
Lord, in these latter days, make me a fountain of blessing to those around me. I so look forward to being with You someday.

Enjoy What You Do

When the enemy shall come in like a flood, the Spirit of the Lord shall lift up a standard against him.

ISAIAH 59:19 (KJV)

I love Proverbs 31:15 (TLB). It simply says: "She gets up before dawn to prepare breakfast for her household and plans the day's work..."

One of the secrets of success is to enjoy whatever you do—not just for yourself, but for the satisfaction of giving of yourself to others in love. And where better than in the kitchen!

Make food preparation a ministry of love. In the Bible, mealtimes or feasts were often celebrations. Perk up your dinners by serving your family a new dish each week if possible.

Notice what your family enjoys at restaurants, and try to duplicate the dishes at home.

Ask family members to list their favorite dishes, then compile menus around those recipes.

If you think you just don't have the energy to be creative, try going to bed earlier for a few nights and "get up before dawn." I believe the Lord gives something extra to those who rise early and do it as unto the Lord.

Simple Pleasures

* Plan a leisurely Saturday breakfast that lasts until noon.
* Try stretching slowly and feeling muscles awaken slowly.
* Display daisies.

Wisdom for Living

Good morning, Lord. There is so much to be done today.
But nothing is more important to me than doing it with You.
I'm ready to begin. Show me the way.

A Harvest of Memories

Whither thou goest, I will go; and where thou lodgest, I will lodge: thy people shall be my people, and thy God my God.

RUTH 1:16 (KJV)

Traveling through life is quite an adventure. Family car trips are no exception. When summer rolls around, there's nothing quite as fun as a family outing to some nearby or faraway destination. Your travel plans can bring your family many happy traditions and lasting memories, but you've got to *keep it simple!*

Carry a small cooler with snacks and drinks. Make lunch a picnic. If you have small children, try taking colored pencils and a sharpener instead of crayons. They won't melt! Make sure each child has a large clipboard and a big pad of drawing paper so there'll be no arguing. Regularly switch seats. Stop often to stretch, go to the restroom, and get a snack and beverage.

Stop driving in the early afternoon so the family can enjoy the swimming pool at the motel. Put a sheet in the backseat over the seat and floor to catch all the crumbs and trash. When you come to a stop, take out the sheet and put the debris in a trash can.

Family outings are times to enjoy one another! Plan a trip today!

Simple Pleasures

- Treat yourself to blueberries and cream.
- Add fresh hot, buttery corn to your patio dinner.
- Piping hot shortcake with strawberries and whipped cream on top makes a wonderful dessert.

Wisdom for Living

As we travel, Lord, I'll need patience. The journey is long. Give me the grace to make it fun and uplifting for others along the way.

A Cornucopia of Pleasures

The way of an eagle in the air; the way of a serpent upon a rock; the way of a ship in the midst of the sea; and the way of a man with a maid.

Proverbs 30:19 (KJV)

Life is full of simple pleasures that bring calm to our spirits and delight to our senses. Here are some reminders of the simple pleasures of life!

The sun on the back of your neck. Dawn. The smell of bacon or coffee first thing in the morning, or chocolate chip cookies when you come in the door in the afternoon. Singing in church. Making a new friend. Finding money in the couch. Getting into a freshly made bed.

Making someone smile. Getting a tax refund or a great haircut. Moonlight on the ocean. The smell of freshly mowed grass. Having exact change. Fishing with your dad. Pink slippers. Watching your kids when they're sleeping. The sound of rain on the roof—especially when you're under the covers. Licking the frosting bowl. Wearing something new. Browsing in a bookstore.

Two scoops! Being excited about tomorrow.

Today, listen to the wisdom found in Psalm 116:6: "The LORD preserves the simple." Don't miss the abundance of simple pleasures in every day.

Simple Pleasures

A garden is a place where little miracles occur every moment.

—Sue Muszala

Wisdom for Living

I bask in Your goodness, Lord. I wonder at the world You have created for me to live in. You are a great God. I'm looking for Your simple pleasures today.

The Power of the Negative

He maketh the storm a calm, so that the waves thereof are still. Then are they glad because they be quiet; so he bringeth them unto their desired haven.

PSALM 107:29-30 (KJV)

What is it that sometimes keeps us from doing the things we really need to do? We have all experienced the frustration of that project we just can't seem to get to. It slowly turns from the thing we keep putting off to the thing we absolutely dread doing! Let's see if we can break that logjam.

Make a list of three things you need to do. Beside each item, write two reasons why you're *not* doing it.

Once you identify what's holding you back, attempt to rethink the situation and change the two negatives into two positives. The ability to turn a negative attitude into a positive one is the key to self-organization.

For instance, one of the biggest reasons people put off accomplishing their goals is because the project as a whole is too overwhelming. If this is one of your main obstacles, rethink the project and break it down into small, manageable steps that seem more like fun than drudgery.

Do it now. Turn those negative roadblocks into positive stepping-stones.

Simple Pleasures

* Take a risk; change something.
* Act in some way you've never acted before.
* Be bold, but kind.

Wisdom for Living

Little by little, You are conforming me into the image of Your Son, dear Father. Reveal Yourself to me today in the obstacles I face. Show me Your way; give me Your peace.

Finding God in a Garden

Now the Lord God had planted a garden in the east, in Eden; and there he put the man he had formed.

GENESIS 2:8

Let me encourage you to make children a real part of your life and home. Just remember, *keep it simple!* Make your home a learning lab for your children!

Most children love the outdoors. My grandchildren are out the door the minute the opportunity presents itself. Even a tiny yard can provide any child with a place to explore and have fun. It doesn't take much to provide an outdoor play area for children. A few sturdy plastic yard toys from a garage sale will say to a child, "I care about you, too."

Better yet, put on your gardening togs and invite a child to come work with you in your garden. Find a piece of ground where they can dig the soil. Provide them with a selection of flower or vegetable seeds and just watch their faces light up with delight.

As you share time in the garden, you will be establishing a space where the generations live and work and learn together. This is where one generation can teach another about life, beauty, the things of God, and how He loves them.

Simple Pleasures

The bluebird carries the sky on his back.

—HENRY DAVID THOREAU

Wisdom for Living

Flowers, colors, textures, rain, sunshine, water, soil. You are the wonderful Creator-God. Produce Your love and goodness in me.

We All Love the Word "Comfortable"

> And I will ask the Father, and he will give you another Counselor to be with you forever.
>
> JOHN 14:16

Whether you're in your home every day or work outside the home, your kitchen has got to be just right! Since the kitchen is the heart of the home for many families, it's important that each family member from the oldest down to the youngest feels comfortable in this center of your home. Here are some ideas for comfortable kitchens.

Let your kitchen décor change with the season: delicate, new fruits and flowers in spring; a colorful bounty of produce in summer; golden-colored pumpkins and chrysanthemums in fall; Christmas reds and greens in winter.

Tuck a tiny lamp in a high cabinet with glass doors to showcase some pretty mugs or serving pieces. Pretty cotton dish towels make beautiful napkins, placemats—or even café curtains! Or try sewing several together and hanging them across the top of your window to form a cheerful valance. Display fruit—or even vegetables—in a basket or special bowl on the kitchen table.

Make your kitchen not only comfortable, but a place of comfort as well.

Simple Pleasures

If I can put one touch of rosy sunset into the life of any man or woman, I shall feel that I have worked with God.

—GEORGE McDONALD

Wisdom for Living

You are the God of all comfort. Give me grace to share Your comfort with others today.

A Healthy Garden

Build houses and settle down; plant gardens and eat what they produce.

JEREMIAH 29:28

Wouldn't you love to have visited the first garden God created? It must have been beautiful—fragrant, lush, and green, yet ordered and balanced. When I think of my garden at home, I often think of my life. Does it reflect that same beauty, order, and abundance that God created in His first garden? I hope so.

Let your garden be a part of your home. It's amazing how the two can work together to create the atmosphere that speaks of God's simplicity and balance. Gardening lets us participate in God's process of creation. A well-cared-for garden goes hand in hand with a well-cared-for life!

Simple Pleasures

No ray of sunshine is ever lost, but the green
which it awakens into existence needs time to sprout,
and it is not always granted for the sower to see the harvest.
All work that is worth anything is done in faith.

—ALBERT SCHWEITZER

Wisdom for Living

My heart's desire is to praise Your name, Lord. Order my steps today that my life will show forth Your glory and Your goodness.

The Heritage of the Kitchen

When you enter a house, first say,
"Peace to this house."

LUKE 10:5

My dear father had an interesting upbringing. As an orphan in pre-war Austria, my father spent much of his time in the kitchen of a palace where he learned the art of cooking. Later, when he immigrated to America, he opened many fine restaurants and even worked for Fox Studios in Hollywood during the 1940s.

Much of my own young childhood was spent in kitchens, as well. The kitchen was always where I wanted to be. It was a place where meals and memories were created.

Later, after my father died and my mother and I lived behind her little dress shop, the kitchen was still the center of warmth. I remember so often being welcomed home with a baked potato, hot cocoa, cinnamon apples, or toasty popovers—all simple expressions of my mother's love!

Even today, the kitchen feels like the heart of the home to me. As Proverbs 17:1 says, "Better a dry crust with peace and quiet than a house full of feasting, with strife."

Your kitchen can be the heart of your home. Start with peace and quiet.

Simple Pleasures

- Brighten the dining room with an indoor window box of impatiens.
- Plant a row of herb plants on the kitchen window.
- If you have a porch, fill an attractive wheeled cart with red geraniums.

Wisdom for Living

Dear Lord, allow Your Spirit to speak peace through me
this day to a wounded world. By Your stripes we are healed.
Let Your healing come to those who seek Your face.

September

REINVENTING YOUR LIFE

Just Around the Corner

We all, with open face beholding as in a glass the glory of the Lord, are changed into the same image…

2 CORINTHIANS 3:18 (KJV)

You never know what opportunities may lie just around the corner! One thing is for sure—God delights to bless us with the adventure of walking with Him day by day. Step-by-step He reveals His amazing plan for our lives. Here's a story of how God blessed my son, Brad, in ways he couldn't have imagined!

Brad and a friend of his came across a duplex that was a real dump! The only thing this property in southern California had going for it was its close proximity to the beach. For two young guys it was perfect. After years of fixing it up, their hard work paid off—they were offered twice what they'd paid for it by a local developer.

Instead of selling it, however, they decided to develop the property themselves. They tore down the building and built two separate three-story units, complete with ocean views! Homes to bring their brides to someday! Today, our son and his wife, Maria, have a lovely beach house with a modern, warm, homey feel.

As images of the Creator, we have the opportunity to fashion our lives and our homes into works of art!

Simple Pleasures

* Sip a glass of grapefruit juice while you bathe.
* Start a savings account for weekend getaways. Research as you save.
* Purchase a roll of stamps and a pretty holder. It's great to be prepared.

Wisdom for Living

Change me, God. I long to be changed. And while You're changing me, make me patient—I know it takes time to create something truly beautiful!

Second Chances

The Lord will perfect that which concerneth me: thy mercy, O Lord, endureth for ever: forsake not the works of thine own hands.

PSALM 138:8 (KJV)

I love my garden. I find such pleasure in the beauty of the plants and flowers. But it also speaks to me of God's love and His incredible patience with me. In a garden, God always gives you a second chance. With time, patience, and fertilizer, even major mistakes can be corrected and loveliness can result.

Take a moment to take stock of your living space. There are so many ways to cultivate the spirit of a garden in your home. Where can you use flowers and plants to decorate your home? A brass pot of zinnias on the coffee table? A container of philodendron to brighten a dark corner of your family room? Do you have an entry hall? It's the perfect spot for a vase of freshly picked roses to welcome family and guests. Make liberal use of houseplants. God's greenery pleases the eye and soothes the spirit. He planned it that way.

Today, find room for a garden in your life. It will serve as a good reminder of how gracious the Lord is toward those who put their trust in Him. His goal is your loveliness!

Simple Pleasures

- A good-looking mat at your front and back doors adds a touch of class.
- Set up a work space with a personal touch—gold or multicolored paperclips.
- Keep a flower on your desk; always a flower.

Wisdom for Living

The garden of my life seems dry today. Please refresh me, Lord, by Your Spirit. Let me walk in the confidence that I am loved.

Our Work Is Never Done

The ants are a people not strong, yet they prepare their meat in the summer.

PROVERBS 30:25 (KJV)

Life can be overwhelming. Let's make it our goal to *keep it simple*.

My Bob and I were returning home one afternoon from doing errands and our route took us over a giant bridge. Bob started to tell me how the workers on this bridge never finish their work. That sounded familiar! He went on to tell me that as soon as the maintenance personnel finish chipping away the rust and painting this engineering marvel, they have to start all over again. Their work is never done.

As homemakers, we're faced with the same problem. When it comes to taking care of our homes, there's always something needing repair, replacement, renovation, or something!

Today, grasp the truth that life is a process and our homes are in process. God intended us to live and grow, and growth is a process. Hang in there, keep it simple, and be flexible. As you do the dishes for the third time today, be grateful that you have dishes to wash!

Simple Pleasures

- Perfume your writing paper by spraying a fragrance inside the box.
- Use pretreated pinecones to add color and scent to your next fire.
- Put on jogging shoes and clean house to some fast-paced music.

Wisdom for Living

Overwhelmed! Lord, that is an understatement today!
Please calm my heart and my mind. Bring stillness to my troubled waters.
I will rest in Your peace today!

Minimum Daily Adult Requirement

My grace is sufficient for thee: for my strength is made perfect in weakness. Most gladly therefore will I rather glory in my infirmities, that the power of Christ may rest upon me.

2 CORINTHIANS 12:9 (KJV)

Isn't it just like us to do what will satisfy the requirements and no more? How we sometimes wish we could know what the "minimum daily adult requirement" is for being a believer in Christ!

Amazingly, the Scriptures set a standard that knows no bounds. God's Word challenges us to be like Christ. An impossibility for every one of us. After all, Jesus was perfect—perfectly God and perfect as a man when He walked this earth.

So, how can we become more like our Lord and Savior? First, if we're to grow to be like the Lord, we need to study to see what He did and how He did it. Jesus studied to show Himself approved. He knew the Old Testament record and studied the Law of Moses. As you read the New Testament, you see Him meeting with others who were seeking the things of God. He prayed regularly. And He responded to those around Him who were in need. It pleased Jesus to do these things.

List in your journal some activities that will help you grow in the Lord; things you would be pleased to do. Then do them. Simply stated, this is grace and not law!

Simple Pleasures

Life is a long lesson in humility.

—JAMES BARRIE

Wisdom for Living

Grace, Lord. What would I do without Your grace? Humble me so that I might receive more of Your grace. Break me so that I can be made whole.

187

A Heritage from the Lord

You are not your own; you were bought at a price. Therefore honor God with your body.

1 CORINTHIANS 6:19-20

In a recent Bible study, the teacher asked us, "Did you feel loved by your parents when you were a child?" Many said, "No, they were too busy for me." "Yes, but I spent too much time with the babysitters." "I don't know. I always seemed to be in their way. I wasn't important to them."

I was amazed at how many grown women expressed reasons they felt unloved in their homes growing up. What would your answer be?

A home should be a place where its members come to be rejuvenated from busy days and demanding schedules. Your home should reflect the quiet and peaceful atmosphere that allows the human spirit to be restored and refreshed.

Say no when you're tempted to just become the family taxi driver. Children will take their cues from you. It's time to show them that God has a better plan. He wants us to walk in His ways.

Stop and take time to listen to your children—eye to eye. Slow down the pace of life long enough to let each child know that they are seen and known. Give your child a beautiful gift today—*time!* It's a heritage they won't forget.

Simple Pleasures

The happiest heart that ever beat
Was in some quiet breast
That found the common daylight sweet
And left to Heaven the rest.

—JOHN V. CHENEY

Wisdom for Living

Lord, You said in the Psalms that when my mother or father forsake me, You will take me up. Thank You for being there for me always.

Mirror Image

Let us fix our eyes on Jesus, the author and perfecter of our faith, who for the joy set before him endured the cross, scorning its shame, and sat down at the right hand of the throne of God.

HEBREWS 12:2

One of the most common decorating techniques is what designers call clustering. But don't mistake *clustering* for *cluttering*. The goal is focus—create a focal point for any room and give it visual appeal.

A large room with a very open design can easily have a number of cluster points that catch the eye. A fireplace can become a point around which furniture or collections of photographs or books can cluster to create wonderful focal point. A simple large mirror or painting and a few candlesticks will also do the trick.

In fact, using mirrors is really one of my favorite ways to make a beautifully dramatic focus for any room. An old beat-up mirror with a frame can look striking, when it's arranged over a little bench with a potted plant or a bowl of potpourri.

First Corinthians 13:12 (NASB) says, "For now we see in a mirror dimly, but then face to face; now I know in part, but then I will know fully just as I also have been fully known." Mirrors always remind me that someday I will see things as they really are. Until that day comes, focus your rooms by clustering, and see if mirrors can help.

Simple Pleasures

* Place small rugs on your closet floors. It helps with dust and adds color!
* Notice light reflected on the wall as it streams through window shutters.
* Make fluffy bubbles and enjoy the colors of the rainbow in your bathtub.

Wisdom for Living

Lord, I need to see the way things really are right now. I need to know the truth. Help me to see clearly according to Your truth.

Don't Be a Paperwork Slave

Who gave himself for us, that he might redeem us from all iniquity, and purify unto himself a peculiar people, zealous of good works.

TITUS 2:14 (KJV)

Paper may be the bane of our existence. If you've ever felt this way, it's time to wise up about paper. If you find yourself buried in years of collected or forgotten papers, there's hope! Let's get rid of the paper!

Start with the room that annoys you the most. Work your way through every pile of paper, newspaper, magazines, or children's schoolwork. Go through closets and drawers. When you finish a room, move on to the next.

Throw it away! Be determined. Make decisions. Throw away the clutter. Save a minimum of papers. Put the throwaways into bags and carry them to the trash. Don't wait. It's a good feeling.

Now, one last piece of advice, and it may be the most important one of all: don't get bogged down rereading and reminiscing. Old letters, old recipes, old articles. It's just that—old.

Someone once said, "Next to the dog, the wastebasket is man's best friend!" Keep your heart and mind focused on freedom and simplicity.

Simple Pleasures

- Any daily ritual can be deeply satisfying and enjoyable. Find new ways to enjoy old tasks.
- Take it to heart, life is principally a matter of paying attention to detail.
- Artichokes are yummy with dips like warm butter or cold mayonnaise. Delectable!

Wisdom for Living

It's time to clean up my act. Out with the old!
A new season has come. Thank You, Lord, for the change of seasons, for the chance to start again. I'm ready.

Treat Yourself to Better Health

He makes me lie down in green pastures, he leads me beside quiet waters, he restores my soul.

PSALM 23:2

Have you ever considered allowing yourself the luxury of doing nothing? We have so much trouble justifying such a thing, don't we? But that's exactly what you need to do sometimes—*nothing!*

For your physical and spiritual health, you need to take vacations and an occasional long lunch hour when you can. Listen to your body. When it tells you that you're exhausted, don't schedule new activities.

Take time to rest. Soak in a bubble bath or read a good book. Try very hard not to bring your work home. It will be there tomorrow.

Human beings tolerate stress and pressure much more easily if at least one person knows they're enduring it. Let a good friend pray with you—talk about what's on your mind and in your schedule.

When you're tired, you're attacked by ideas that you thought you conquered long ago. Don't give the enemy a place in your life to land. Let the Lord restore your peace of mind today.

Simple Pleasures

- Find a comfortable mat and do 30 minutes of stretching exercises to music or a video.
- Replace old photographs of children and cherished friends with new ones.
- Color-code your file folders with a different color for each day of the week.

Wisdom for Living

Jesus, lead me beside still waters. Gentle Shepherd, restore my soul. I am willing to be led, and I need Your restoring touch on my life.

What You Know

For in the time of trouble he shall hide me in his pavilion: in the secret of his tabernacle shall he hide me; he shall set me up upon a rock.

PSALM 27:5 (KJV)

"I sought the LORD, and he answered me;
   he delivered me from all my fears...
This poor [woman] called, and the LORD heard [me];
   he saved [me] out of all [my] troubles...
Taste and see that the LORD is good;
   blessed is the [woman] who takes refuge in him."

Those beautiful words from Psalm 34:4,6,8 constantly remind me of what I already know. How about you? Could you use some reminding?

Today, remember that what you *know* is more important than how you *feel*. If you feel fearful, claim God's promise that He will never leave you or forsake you. If you are depressed and downhearted, claim the joy that He promises to give to every one of us who name His name. If you can't seem to find your way, trust that the God who has never let you down will be there for you today.

For You, O Lord, are my hope when my spirit's weak. I know you're with the brokenhearted who believe in You. I will trust You, for You encourage me. I have no fear of what's ahead of me. The eyes of the Lord are forever upon me.

Simple Pleasures

Christianity is a battle, not a dream.

—WENDELL PHILLIPS

Wisdom for Living

I live before You, Father. You are the source of my life. Today, I will trust You more. I choose to trust You more.

Broken Dreams

And the floors shall be full of wheat, and the fats shall overflow with wine and oil. And I will restore to you the years that the locust hath eaten…

JOEL 2:24-25 (KJV)

In these past years when I've felt so broken and worn, I've wondered if my heavenly Father finds joy in restoring me. After all, restoration is exactly what He promises us through Scripture. "He restores my soul," sings the psalmist. "The God of all grace, who called you to his eternal glory in Christ…will himself restore you," says Peter.

My heart cries out, "What are you going to do, Lord? I need a bit of a miracle right about now." It gives me such great pleasure to know that some of my own pain and suffering can be an encouragement to you today.

Will we be healed? Absolutely. I can't say precisely how it will happen. The Scriptures tell us that by the Lord's mercy, we *are* being healed, being made perfect, in a process that will take an entire lifetime—and perhaps longer—to complete.

Regardless of how long it takes, His promise is sure: He will complete the work begun in you. He will finish the work He started. He will bring you into wholeness; if not in this life, in the next!

Simple Pleasures

- Share your homemade chicken stock with a neighbor who is ill.
- Jot a note today using note cards or interesting museum postcards.
- A selection of stamps adds a personal touch to your correspondence.

Wisdom for Living

O God, how will things ever be right again? I am broken, and healing seems a long way off. I know Your promises are true. I need Your grace to believe.

The Joy of Learning to Lean

> *For ye have need of patience, that, after ye have done the will of God, ye might receive the promise.*
>
> HEBREWS 10:36 (KJV)

I hope you're learning to lean! What exactly am I talking about? It's something that I've been working on for quite some time now.

I've always been a can-do kind of person. I manage my time well. I keep my commitments. *I can!* That is, until recently, when I found myself saying over and over, "I can't. I just can't." What happens when you can't do any more, or when you can't do something in particular that you once could?

I know the answer now, though it's taken me several painful years. When you reach a certain point, you learn to lean—on your family, your friends, and especially on the Lord. In the process, you receive the priceless gift of realizing how much you are loved and cared for.

More valuable than that, you receive the gift of recognizing your own weakness. You learn how to "cast your cares on him," knowing He cares for you. Learning to lean came hard for me. But it has been one of the most valuable lessons of a difficult season in my life!

Simple Pleasures

* Choose a personal journal style with a colorful or distinctive blank book.
* Make a long-distance call you've been putting off.
* Keep a running reading and movie list. Keep it with you.

Wisdom for Living

Dear Lord, I know it will be easier to open my life to others if I first open more to You. I'm casting my cares on You, Lord. Thank You that You care.

Links in the Blessing Chain

Praying always with all prayer and supplication in the Spirit, and watching thereunto with all perseverance and supplication for all saints.

EPHESIANS 6:18 (KJV)

To be honest, I have to admit it. There's a part of me that would absolutely love to hang it all up and retire. So why don't I quit, as so many friends have been asking me to do? Do you ever feel like calling it quits, even if you're not close to retirement age? What keeps us going in moments like those?

As I've actually contemplated retiring, I've come to realize that in my heart of hearts, I'm just not ready yet, or more accurately, that God just isn't finished with me yet. When I see the wonderful, exciting things that He is doing, I find confirmation and encouragement to press on. When I see His hand at work in the lives of those around me, I know that my work is not finished.

The Lord is doing a good work. I want to be a witness for what He has done for me—and for what He wants to do for *you*. I want to share my hurts so that you will feel liberated to share yours.

We all can be a link in God's wonderful chain of blessing in the world. And so I'm not ready to quit—at least not yet! How about you?

Simple Pleasures

- Get a lined notepad and record new words and their definitions.
- Keep a good dictionary right by your reading chair.
- Learn a new language with tapes or on the Internet.

Wisdom for Living

Thank You, Lord, for the call You have placed on my life. I want my life to be a blessing not only to others, but also to You today.

Quietly Wrestling

O sing to the Lord a new song,
For He has done wonderful things,
His right hand and His holy arm
have gained the victory for Him.

PSALM 98:1 (NASB)

To me, the words "quiet time" bring images of sitting in a cozy window seat, reading the Bible, and praying. And of course, there's a wonderfully fragrant cup of tea steaming at my elbow! My vision includes my journal and a heart full of gratitude as I record all of God's blessings and the wonderful things I know He's teaching me.

However, as you are enjoying this image with me, I have to confess— my quiet times aren't always so quiet, or so joyful! Sometimes these daily times with the Lord are more like a silent wrestling match as I struggle with my fears, my worries, my pain. I come to these times distracted and confused, sometimes filled with anxiety as I contemplate my day. But isn't that why we need a quiet time in the first place? It's so simple when you think about it.

My quiet time is not a gift I give to God. It's a gift *God* gives to *me!* I come to Him with my cup of confusion and worry. He takes the cup, empties it, and then pours into it His fullness, His quietness, and His peace.

Whether it's quiet or not, find time for a quiet time today.

Simple Pleasures

- Rotate books and magazines. Refresh the visual images.
- Try a superior quality furniture polish on cherished wood pieces.
- Buy several photo scrapbooks so you're ready for new photos.

Wisdom for Living

Lord, I need victory. The enemy of my soul is formidable. But I know that Your Word is true: greater is He that is in me, than he that is in the world.

First Impressions

He put a new song in my mouth,
a hymn of praise to our God.
Many will see and fear and put
their trust in the Lord.

PSALM 40:3

Our mothers often told us, "It's the first impression that counts." That can apply, of course, to more than just how you act or dress. It can also apply to your home and how people feel as they approach it. With a little thought and a little caring, you can have a home that makes guests and family alike feel instantly at home. Where do you begin? In a sense, you begin at the door—or even at the curb.

A whimsical mailbox by the driveway, for instance, can say a happy hello to anyone who approaches. A bright banner hanging in the apartment hallway announces, "This is the right place and we want you in it!" Brightly colored flowers tell your visitor that this is a happy place and "We're happy you're here."

More importantly, though, you begin your first impression with what the Bible describes as a hospitable heart. You begin with a willingness to share your life—to make space in your plans for friends, family, and strangers. It's not easy in our busy day and age. But it's still true—first impressions count!

Simple Pleasures

One flower at a time. I want to hear what it is saying.

—ROBERT FRANCIS FROM "BOUQUETS"

Wisdom for Living

Lord, I want others' first impression of my life to be that I belong to You. Thank You for rescuing me from the miry pit and setting me on the Rock.

Coffee Tables and Fellowship

Make every effort to live in peace with all men and to be holy; without holiness no one will see the Lord.

HEBREWS 12:14

Do you remember the days when neighbors frequently invited each other over for coffee or stood at the back fence and visited for an hour? Lingering has become something of a lost art in our society.

Europeans still know how to linger. You can sit in their coffee houses for hours nursing a small cappuccino and no one will think twice about it.

Spending time together lays a foundation for harmony between family members and friends. When we are too busy to stop and smell the roses, it's a lot easier to find ourselves snipping at one another or being caught in some misunderstanding.

Romans 12:16 says, "Live in harmony with one another." That means blending together, finding time to mesh our lives with one another. It means finding time around a coffee table or at a local coffee house to really hear and say the things that come from our hearts.

Today, meet a friend for a coffee break or better yet, invite someone over for tea.

Simple Pleasures
- Enjoy not setting your alarm on Saturday mornings.
- Stretch out for a nap in front of the fireplace on Sunday afternoon.
- Treat your family to the smell of pot roast when returning home from church.

Wisdom for Living
I don't know how to slow down, Lord, but I know You do. Show me.

White Spaces

I have set before you life and death, blessings and curses. Now choose life, so that you and your children may live.

DEUTERONOMY 30:19

What would we women do without our daily planners? I have a friend who just got her first planner, and you'd think the idea was invented yesterday! She is so excited to finally get her life organized! I don't know how a person functions today without some type of organizer.

For years I loved my busy calendar. It made me feel alive, plugged in, and productive. Then one day I came upon a page that had all white space and I panicked. What would I do to fill the time? That's how I used to think!

Today, life has become more complicated and complex. I rarely come across a day filled with white space. In fact, now I actually plan my "white spaces" as part of my weekly, monthly, and yearly planning. These white spaces represent days that are saved for me and my family. These days are precious times for me and those I love.

Ecclesiastes 3:1 (NASB) says, "There is an appointed time for everything. And there is a time for every event under heaven." Begin to control your calendar. Make time for your God, yourself, your loved ones. Make those white spaces your friend!

Simple Pleasures

Dost thou love life? Then do not squander time,
for that is the stuff that life is made of.

—BENJAMIN FRANKLIN

Wisdom for Living

O God, time is short and we must make the most of it. Yet, I need those quiet moments when I can contemplate Your goodness and be renewed in my spirit. Show me how to find that balance today, Lord.

Unclutter Your Clutter

But I fear, lest by any means, as the serpent beguiled Eve through his subtlety, so your minds should be corrupted from the simplicity that is in Christ.

2 CORINTHIANS 11:3 (KJV)

Suppose I said to you today, "I want to go through every one of your closets, open every drawer, and peek under every bed." You'd probably say, "No way! You're not going to inspect my mess!"

Well, take that mess, clean it up, and rest! Commit yourself to a five-week program to unclutter your clutter. Does five weeks not seem like enough time? You'll be so surprised at what you can accomplish in five weeks. Here we go!

First, work this plan one small portion at a time. Target one room a week for the next five weeks, and take that one room in easy, manageable, 15-minute time slots.

Go into room one and clean like mad for 15 minutes. Now forget it until the next day, and then do the same thing again, cleaning and organizing. Continue the process throughout the week. Presto! By week's end, you'll have one of those rooms cleaned and organized!

Room by room, the Lord will see you through. Get ready, go!

Simple Pleasures

- Go outside to see myriads of stars in a moonlit sky.
- Notice cardinals flashing across green and blue.
- Watch squirrels digging everywhere, storing nuts for winter's descent.

Wisdom for Living

Dear Jesus, it's as simple as saying, "I do." I do want to honor You. I do want to follow You. I will seek Your face this day.

The Importance of the Basics

Like newborn babies, crave pure spiritual milk, so that by it you may grow up in your salvation.

1 PETER 2:2

I'm always distressed when I find children who haven't been taught the basics. As any parent knows, it's not always easy. Nevertheless, there are simple basics that must be taught and learned if children are to become healthy adults.

The biblical admonition states, "Train a child in the way he should go, and when he is old he will not turn from it." This is true not only for their spiritual lives, but it also applies to what they learn to do around the house.

Even a five-year-old can learn to set the table. It amazed me when our daughter would bring her teenage friends home and they didn't even know how to set a table. It wasn't their fault. Mom or Dad never took the time to teach them. As your five-year-old sets the table you can say, "Okay, Chad, do whatever you want. You can use the good china or paper plates; you can have candlelight, or you can put your favorite teddy bear on the table."

This is a simple illustration, but without a proper foundation, children will be handicapped for future endeavors. God knows the same thing applies to us!

Simple Pleasures

Every man is a volume, if you know how to read him.

—WILLIAM CHANNING

Wisdom for Living

I humble myself before You, heavenly Father. Don't let me miss the things I so need to learn to be effective in Your kingdom. This is my prayer.

Wake-up Call

> Blow ye the trumpet in Zion, and sound an alarm in my holy mountain: let all the inhabitants of the land tremble: for the day of the Lord cometh, for it is nigh at hand.

JOEL 2:1 (KJV)

The wake-up hour comes pretty early during the school year. Are your mornings hectic and confused, or is there peace and quiet as you prepare for the day? Help your children each morning by setting a tone of love and serenity that will follow them throughout their day. Here are a few practical tips!

What do you do when you have breakfast ready and no one comes to the table when they are called? Isn't that irritating? It bothered me so much that we finally called a family meeting and asked them, "What are we going to do?" One of them said to me, "Mom, if you'd just let us know a couple of minutes before breakfast, we'd come right to the table." Now, that's exactly what we do!

At your home, try ringing a chime, playing the piano, singing a song, or blowing a whistle—whatever works! Give them a warning and they'll come. Could it be that simple? It worked beautifully in our family.

Once they are there, thank the Lord for all that He's provided, and speak His blessing over your precious family!

Simple Pleasures

* Create Chore Charts for keeping track of daily progress and rewards.
* Thank God for the opportunity to spend money when it's appropriate.
* Value your saving accounts.

Wisdom for Living

Sound the trumpet in Zion—and through my life—that You reign on high and in all the affairs of men. Hallelujah!

Don't Pile It, File It!

You need to persevere so that when you have done the will of God, you will receive what he has promised.

HEBREWS 10:36

Looking for a new motto to encourage your home organization efforts? Then give mine a try: Don't pile it, file it.

This principle will really tidy up your life. Go to your local stationery store and purchase about four dozen file folders. I like colored ones because they're brighter and add some cheer to my day. Plus, they always look more fun than those plain vanilla ones. I actually *want* to work with them most of the time!

On your folders, use simple headings: Sales Tax, Auto, Insurance, School Papers, Maps, Warranties, Taxes, Checks, etc. Think of any category that produces paper over the course of a year.

Then take all those loose papers around your home and put them in their proper place. If you have a file cabinet, that's great. If not, pick up a cardboard storage box to get started.

Don't you feel better already? Borrow my motto and watch it work for you!

Simple Pleasures

- Do something fun with a tax refund.
- Make use of two-for-one coupons for coffee or a shared meal.
- Keep a collection of road maps tucked neatly in a side pocket in your car.

Wisdom for Living

Your promises are the foundation of my life, Father. Thank You that Your promises will be accomplished in this world and in my life. Hallelujah!

The Risky Business of Talent

Wherefore I put thee in remembrance that thou stir up the gift of God...For God hath not given us the spirit of fear; but of power, and of love, and of a sound mind.

2 TIMOTHY 1:6-7 (KJV)

As a child growing up behind my mother's dress shop store, I had no idea God could use me for much. It wasn't until many years later that God challenged me to take small steps to venture out into this world of risks.

We wish that our talents came out full-grown, but they don't. It's only as we cultivate them that they become mature. Listen to God— He's calling you to a life of adventure.

Do you have a song to be sung, a book to be authored? We must be willing to be used, to take risks.

But, you may wonder, how do I start? Start by asking your heavenly Father to reveal to you those special gifts He placed within you and that He wants to develop in you. Another good way to ascertain what special gifting you might have is to ask a trusted friend to share her perception of your talents.

Then develop your plan and create a timetable to begin using these talents and gifts for the Lord. Be a risk-taker!

Simple Pleasures

I will study and get ready, and perhaps my chance will come.

—ABRAHAM LINCOLN

Wisdom for Living

Courage, Lord, I need courage. There are great things to be done. Dreams You have put in my heart. Show me, Lord, what to do next. I only want to follow You.

October

SEASONS OF THE SOUL

The Discipline of Time

*Be still, and know that I am God:
I will be exalted among the
heathen, I will be exalted in the
earth.*

PSALM 46:10 (KJV)

Time is a precious commodity, no doubt about it! We never feel we have enough of it, and most of us struggle all our lives with how to use it wisely. It's a worthy goal, therefore, to understand how time works best for you, and then to work hard at implementing that understanding.

Discover the time of day when you feel at your best and schedule important activities to fall into that time period. Start your daily tasks with what matters; then do the quick, easy, and enjoyable jobs to build up momentum.

One of the best ways I have found to maximize my time and stay true to my priorities is to learn to say no. It's a hard word to say at times, but so valuable. We live in a society that prides itself on being busy, but as someone once said, "The main thing is to keep the main thing the main thing." Try it.

Lastly, don't fill more than 75 percent of your day. Save some time for the unexpected—for one of God's surprises! Save time for a moment of quiet between you and the Lord.

Simple Pleasures

- Try your hand at fly-fishing on a nearby river under autumn leaves.
- Feel the ball when it hits the "sweet spot" on your tennis racket.
- Savor the first pop of popcorn—and the last!

Wisdom for Living

*Father, I humble myself before You this day,
quieting my heart in Your presence. Teach me to recognize You,
when You reveal Yourself in unexpected ways.*

The Right Tools

It is a good thing to give thanks unto the Lord…to shew forth thy lovingkindness in the morning, and thy faithfulness every night.

PSALM 92:1-2 (KJV)

Have you ever struggled to make something work and realized that you just don't have the right tools? Ever ruin your hands on those easy twist-off bottle caps? Try using one of those nutcrackers that lie tucked away in the back of some kitchen drawer. Keep one handy; they make great twist-off bottle cap openers.

Instructions on labels seem to be getting more difficult to read all the time. It's a good idea to keep a magnifying glass nearby. Eliminate eyestrain.

Do your ice-cube trays stubbornly stick to the freezer shelf? Here's an idea: line the freezer shelf with wax paper and you'll never pull at them again.

The psalmist David knew the importance of using the right tool in order to gain understanding.

I will bow down…And give thanks to Your name for Your loving kindness and Your truth; for you have magnified your word…You made me bold with strength in my soul." (Psalm 138:2-3 NASB)

The next time you find yourself in a struggle, lift your voice in praise to a God of wisdom and truth. Praise is always the right tool for the job!

Simple Pleasures

Our life is frittered away by detail…simplify, simplify.

—HENRY DAVID THOREAU

Wisdom for Living

*Dear Lord, I worship You today as the strength of my life.
In all I do, may I show forth Your glory!*

The Spirit of Femininity

Many, O Lord my God, are the wonders which Thou hast done, And Thy thoughts toward us; There is none to compare with Thee; If I would declare and speak of them, They would be too numerous to count.

PSALM 40:5 (NASB)

What's the first thing you do when you pick a rose? You put it to your nose to enjoy the fragrance. How does it make you feel? Maybe it brings a pleasant memory of that little girl inside you or reminds you of someone dear.

Beautiful fragrances around the home are a wonderful way to express our femininity, and you'll be surprised at how much they can contribute to a relaxed and peaceful atmosphere. Put a lavender sachet in your dresser or hang it up in the closet. Boil a little pot of cinnamon and fill your home with a pleasant scent.

There are many delightful fragrance sprays available on the market as well. A fragrant candle burning on the kitchen counter or at your desk is an invitation to a visitor to linger for a moment.

There's nothing self-indulgent about such small, simple pleasures when we approach them with a spirit of gratitude. Think of them as God's gifts to help you go about the tasks He has given you. Cultivate the spirit of femininity and prepare yourself to be God's woman in the world.

Simple Pleasures

- Breathe in the smell of burning wood in the crisp autumn air.
- Smile at boxes and boxes of apples—red, yellow, green.
- Enjoy some crispy cold, fresh-pressed cider.

Wisdom for Living

Thank You, Lord, for giving me the simple pleasures of life. Help me to stop and smell the roses. I don't want life to pass me by just because I am too busy to notice.

Be an Example

As iron sharpens iron, s
sharpens another....As wat
reflects a face, so a man's heart
reflects the man.

PROVERBS 27:17,19

What kind of an example are you? We think it is our words that matter so much with others, but when it comes to influencing those around us, our actions often speak louder than our words.

We teach by example in our homes, at the beach, while jogging, when resting, eating—in every part of the day. You'll find that sons, daughters, grandchildren, nieces, and nephews imitate the values we exhibit in our home.

Little eyes are peering out to see how we behave when no one is looking. Simple things are noticed, like a lighted candle on a table or the "thank you" you offer when food is being served in a restaurant. Are your actions consistent with what you say you believe?

If you believe it is important to be patient, then how do you respond when you're standing in line at the supermarket? If you believe it is important to be a good neighbor, then do you send a quick thank you note for a gift or thoughtful kindness?

We're continually setting some kind of example whether we know it or not. It's as simple as that!

Simple Pleasures

- Catch the fading radiance of summer—autumn's golden glow.
- Leaves, leaves, and more leaves!
- Get your passport renewed.

Wisdom for Living

Thank You for the gift of influence, Lord. I thank You for those who can influence me, and I pray that I might become a person whose influence draws others toward You.

Put a
Ceiling on It

> *He who is full loathes honey, but to the hungry even what is bitter tastes sweet.*
>
> PROVERBS 27:7

The Scriptures encourage us to be content in whatever circumstance we find ourselves. In our "have it all" society this definitely goes against the grain. How can we balance the things we need with the things we want? Over the years, my husband, Bob, and I have learned to put a limit on our desires.

Long ago, we decided together that this is where we stop. We don't need any bigger or better trophies to make us happy. It hasn't always been easy to sort out where to draw the line, especially when there are so many wonderful and inviting things to do and places to go, but God has always rewarded our efforts to do so.

When a family puts a ceiling on their desires, they say to the ones around them, "We can be happy in the present." It means that we are training ourselves to live out the adage that "more isn't always better."

Placing a ceiling on our desires is also a great way to eliminate stress. I can guarantee you, contentment will give you great joy. Make this a matter of prayer and discussion with your family. It's one of the most valuable concepts you can pass along.

Simple Pleasures

To have what we want is riches,
but to be able to do without is power.

— DONALD GRANT

Wisdom for Living

I want You, Lord, and whatever You choose to provide. Give me the grace to let the rest go, and trust You for my real needs.

Refreshing Your Marriage, Refreshing Your Life

*For I am convinced that nei
death, nor life, nor angels,
principalities, nor things pr
nor things to come, nor powers,
nor height, nor depth, nor any
other created thing, shall be able to
separate us from the love of God,
which is in Christ Jesus our Lord.*

ROMANS 8:38-39 (NASB)

When was the last time you had marital solitude? You've got to make it happen—it just doesn't happen otherwise.

For many years now, Bob and I have made it a point to get away from all the noises of life and just be by ourselves. We sleep in. We have no schedules and only limited interruptions. We eat when and if we want.

This is our time to get away from *everything*. It's a wonderful opportunity to rethink life, to write down some individual and joint spiritual goals, and to just have fun together. And don't let excuses sidetrack you.

Start now and set aside a fund for your adventure. Then start planning the date and destination. Get it on your calendar! Bob and I have found that people do what they want to do. Make this a priority and it will happen.

Leave your troubles behind and get away for at least one night. And if you're not married, you can plan the same kind of time either by yourself or with a family member or friend. The important thing is to just do it!

Simple Pleasures

- Take a country drive on a sunny day.
- See if you can feel the tug of a fish on the end of the line.
- Put your garden to bed for winter.

Wisdom for Living

Father, guide me into Your rest.

A Thankful Heart

> For which cause we faint not; but though our outward man perish, yet the inward man is renewed day by day.
>
> 2 CORINTHIANS 4:16 (KJV)

Have you ever noticed how you feel toward someone who has gracious manners and a grateful attitude? I enjoy doing almost anything for a person like that. When favors are expected and unappreciated, it's sometimes a little harder to give.

If that's true for me as a human being, how much more God must be overjoyed when one of His children responds to His many blessings with a thankful heart instead of a demanding one.

There are two kinds of people in the world—the givers and the takers. It seems like today there are more takers than ever before. We desperately need people with hearts and attitudes that are thankful to God.

Jot down in your journal ten things for which you're thankful. Call someone today who means a lot to you and tell her how thankful you are for her friendship. Write a note of thanks to someone today—a friend, a family member, a pastor. Tell God tonight before you go to bed how thankful you are for Him. Be thankful! It's that simple!

Simple Pleasures

A memory without blot or contamination must be an exquisite treasure, an inexhaustible source of pure refreshment.

—CHARLOTTE BRONTË

Wisdom for Living

It's time for renewal! I need to be refreshed, restored, made new! I'm tired, Lord. Pour out Your springs of living water on my tired, weary soul.

Let There Be Light

But ye are a chosen generation, a royal priesthood...that ye should shew forth the praises of him who hath called you out of darkness into his marvellous light.

1 PETER 2:9 (KJV)

If you've ever smiled at someone you love across a warmly lit room, or squinted to read in a dimly lit bedroom, you know how important light can be. The way a room is lit will affect both its comfort and its ambiance.

The sources of light—lamps, chandeliers, candles, and window treatments—are part of your décor, and they're just as important to the visual effect as chairs and paintings. Try to have at least one light source in each corner of a room. Open the curtains and flood your rooms with cheerful sunlight.

Consider this. Jesus knew just how important light was when He said of Himself, "I am the light of the world. Whoever follows me will never walk in darkness, but will have the light of life." Imagine the light source that Jesus can be in your life and mine. Not only did He *create* light, but He *is* the Light of the entire world.

Today, let's praise Him for the light He brings to our lives, and the light He sheds on our paths. Without Him we would still be in darkness. Behold, the darkness has past and the true Light has come.

Simple Pleasures

- Use pink lightbulbs for a softer, warmer glow.
- Stock up on batteries for the coming winter months.
- Light-activated outdoor lamps give comfort and security.

Wisdom for Living

There is darkness here and there in my life, Lord.
Shine Your holy light upon me and wash me white as snow.
I want to be holy even as You are holy.

Plant a Garden

> Thy people also shall be all righteous: they shall inherit the land for ever, the branch of my planting, the work of my hands, that I may be glorified.
>
> ISAIAH 60:21 (KJV)

Gardening doesn't come quite as easily for some of us as it does for others. In fact, I've met women who feel downright intimidated by the thought of planting a garden or even something as simple as a patch of marigolds. Today, I want to encourage you to plant a garden!

Your garden can flourish in whatever space and time you have to give it. In our first apartment, we barely had room for ourselves—and no space for a garden plot. But I was able to cultivate the effect of a garden even in that tiny place. I simply set out small geranium pots in a kitchen window that received early morning sun. Before long, blooms had brightened our little home. That was just the start!

I would occasionally pick up a potted plant in a gallon container. Those little "instant gardens" ended up in the middle of the breakfast table, on the bathroom vanity, and even on the nightstand!

God created the first garden and put the man He formed in it! It was paradise. Today, I encourage you to get a garden!

Simple Pleasures

What is paradise? but a garden, an orchard of trees and herbs full of pleasure and nothing there but delights.

—WILLIAM LAWSON

Wisdom for Living

*You are growing in my heart, Lord Jesus, day by day.
I feel Your strength and Your joy within me. I look forward to
enjoying the beautiful person that You are creating.*

A Role to Play

And he took the children in his arms, put his hands on them and blessed them.

Mark 10:16

Delegating responsibility to children is such an important part of parenting. They are never too young to learn, and it is never too late to start.

Make it fun for them. A three-year-old can dress himself, put her pajamas away, brush his hair, brush her teeth, and make his own bed. Take your little one with you through the home and begin to show him what you're doing. Often children don't even realize that there is toothpaste on the mirror in the bathroom because they've never been taught to wipe it up!

A five-year-old can help clear the table after meals, pick up his room every night, take out some items of recycling, and bring dirty clothes to the laundry room.

A ten-year-old can put the trash out by the curb, help clean out the car on Saturdays, and take care of the younger ones around the house.

Think about it this way. When we begin to delegate responsibilities to our children and allow them to do some of the work for and with us, they begin to sense that they're a vital part of the family. How important that is!

Simple Pleasures

- Take a thermos full of steaming soup to a fall football game.
- Plan a scavenger hunt in the neighborhood.
- Return bottles and cans for a refund.

Wisdom for Living

Oh, how I need Your touch in my life today. I am weary, Lord, from all the comings and goings. Touch me, heal me, and make me whole so that I might serve You more completely.

Home Is Where the Heart Is

The Lord came and stood there, calling as at the other times, "Samuel! Samuel!" Then Samuel said, "Speak, for your servant is listening."

1 SAMUEL 3:10

Are you a good listener? Maybe there is a good reason why God in His great wisdom created us with two ears, and only *one* mouth! I'm sure that was because He wanted us to listen twice as much as we speak. Think about that!

Over the years, my husband, Bob, and I have come to rate the skill of listening as one of the keys to having a good marriage relationship. Remember James 1:19? "Everyone should be quick to listen, slow to speak and slow to become angry." Difficult to do sometimes, but a powerful behavior in any relationship.

One of the things that can motivate us to become better listeners is to realize how much people value being heard. Listening blesses the ones we love by saying loud and clear, "I care about you!" And listening carries a double blessing. Not only do those around us know we care, but our own spirits are lifted up when we know others feel cared for.

Listening is a fine art—it's just as much a creative effort as anything you'll ever do around the house!

Simple Pleasures

The ability to simplify means to eliminate the unnecessary so that the necessary may speak.

—HANS HOFMANN

Wisdom for Living

Teach me today, Lord, to be a better listener. Give me the grace to discipline my heart to quietness and rest before You. I want to hear Your voice above all others.

Our Heavenly Home

The Lord has clothed and girded himself with strength; Indeed, the world is firmly established, it will not be moved.

PSALM 93:1 (NASB)

Maybe one way to think of our homes here on earth is to realize that they can be reflections of the heavenly home we are destined for one day. Our homes can be places of peace and tranquillity. A place where people feel loved.

As much as we love our present home, we believe it belongs to God, not us. Our homes are a rich source of blessing for us and for others.

One way to create a loving atmosphere in your home is by using photos. Family photos are such an easy way of welcoming others into your life. If you have old portraits of Great-Grandma or Uncle Ed, don't hide them—display them for everyone to enjoy.

Cross-stitch or hand-letter a blessing to hang by your front door on the inside, so it speaks to you, your family, and your guests as you go out into the world. A favorite is Numbers 6:24-26:

> The LORD bless you
>   and keep you;
> the LORD make his face shine upon you
>   and be gracious to you;
> the LORD turn his face toward you
>   and give you peace.

Until we go to that heavenly place prepared for us, our homes can reflect a bit of heaven.

Simple Pleasures

- Share fond memories of those departed around the table.
- Remember the birthday of someone whose life touched yours.
- Sing "When the Roll Is Called Up Yonder."

Wisdom for Living

Make me a vessel of Your peace in my home this day.

217

Organized for a Purpose

Prepare the way for the Lord,
make straight paths for him.

MATTHEW 3:3

It's good to stop for a moment and remember the true motivation for getting our lives organized and for following that always relevant advice to *keep it simple*. The purpose, of course, is to allow you more time to spend on the truly important goals in your life—spiritual, physical, emotional, and relational goals.

One of the things that has been helpful for me over the years, and that I still practice diligently is the 45/15 rule. It works like this. After every 45-minute work cycle, I take a 15-minute break and do something different—take a short walk, water a few potted plants, step outside for some fresh air, or return a call or two. I've found that this approach keeps me renewed and refreshed. I return to the next work cycle raring to go!

Here's another idea: assign permanent locations for small, "restless" items, the things that end up on a tabletop or kitchen counter. Just put up a hook near the door for keys, a small dish on the bureau top for loose change or earrings, or a mug on the desk to hold pens and pencils. It's the simple things that work!

Simple Pleasures

- Give someone a good handshake.
- Breathe in the smell of a new car.
- Feel the rain on your face when you don't care if you get wet.

Wisdom for Living

Renew my motivation for getting things in better order, Father.
I just never feel I have enough time for what is important,
and I know I need to be a better steward of my time.

Truly Thankful

Blessing and glory and wisdom and thanksgiving and honor and power and might, be to our God forever and ever. Amen.

REVELATION 7:12 (NASB)

In the wonderful film *The Sound of Music*, Maria bows her head to offer a blessing at her first family meal and prays this simple prayer: "For what we are about to receive, Lord, make us truly thankful!"

Have you ever thought of praying that simple table blessing for all the circumstances of your life? Have you ever thought of asking the Lord to give you the gift of gratitude? It's a gift I've been seeking from the Lord for quite some time. On a daily basis I lift my heart before the Lord and say this prayer: "Lord, for whatever I am receiving and about to receive—pain as well as joy—please teach me the secret of giving thanks."

It isn't always an easy prayer to say with sincerity. In fact, sometimes I feel a little hypocritical when I'm praying it. Sometimes the "thank you" feels a bit reluctant.

Nevertheless, when we pray, "Lord make me truly thankful," we're actually asking for an attitude adjustment! We're asking for a new way of looking at our lives—past, present, and future. It's a prayer worth praying.

Simple Pleasures

- Watch *The Sound of Music*—again!
- See the original *and* the remake of Disney's *The Parent Trap*.
- Watch your father tear up whenever he hears the Marine Corps hymn.

Wisdom for Living

Glory, glory, hallelujah. Glory, glory, hallelujah.

Decorative Ornaments

Nevertheless, God's solid foundation stands firm, sealed with this inscription: "The Lord knows those who are his…"

2 TIMOTHY 2:19

My husband, Bob, and I have had such fun establishing traditions in our family. One of the most meaningful began on our first Christmas together—my very first Christmas as a Christian.

Money was tight that year, but somehow we budgeted for a tree, and treated ourselves by giving each other specially selected ornaments for our little tree.

As our family grew, each child received his or her special ornament on their first Christmas. Even today, our grandchildren each receive an ornament a year, starting with their first.

One year I decided not to give ornaments. After 33 years, I figured nobody cared. How wrong I was! Everybody was so disappointed, I went out the day after Christmas and found just the right ornaments to continue our tradition. It still warms our hearts when we gather together year after year. Even that funny year has become part of this wonderful family tradition.

Traditions add such joy and richness to our lives. After all, the memories of tomorrow are being shaped by the traditions we create today.

Simple Pleasures

As for rosemary…it is the herb sacred to remembrance and friendship, when a sprig of it hath an unspoken language.

—SIR THOMAS MORE

Wisdom for Living

Thank You for memory. For the good memories that are such a blessing. And for the memories that still cause me pain. Lord, heal me and make me whole.

One More "Should"

But the noble man devises noble plans; and by noble plans he stands.

ISAIAH 32:8 (NASB)

Does a quiet time sound like one more *should* in your life—something you ought to be doing but can't seem to manage? When so many depend on you and when so much needs to be done, how can you find the time for a quiet time unless you make it one more *should* in your life?

If any of this sounds familiar, here's the truth: stillness is neither an impossible luxury nor an unreasonable demand—it's a necessity!

You need your quiet time. You need it like you need air, food, sleep, and exercise. Taking care of your inner resources will help you take care of the business of your life. As Isaiah 30:15 puts it,

In repentance and rest is your salvation,
in quietness and trust is your strength.

The people who allow themselves time for stillness make exciting discoveries about God, and about the kind of life God has in mind. Your job is to simply receive it as God's gift to you!

Quiet time isn't a *should,* it's a *must!*

Simple Pleasures

- Shoot a roll of film on leaves, up close and personal.
- Find a four-year-old and jump in a pile of autumn leaves with him.
- Don't miss the smell of leaves burning in fall—it warms the soul.

Wisdom for Living

I need to sort through the shoulds and musts in my life.
I know You will give me the wisdom I need because
You have promised that You will give if I ask. I ask for wisdom, Lord.
Thank You, Lord, for wisdom You are giving me.

A Room for Rest

So they set out from the mountain of the Lord and traveled for three days. The ark of the covenant of the Lord went before them during those three days to find them a place to rest.

NUMBERS 10:33

Have I mentioned how much I love my bedroom? Something of calm and stillness comes over me every time I enter that sacred space. And for me it is sacred, for it's where my husband and I express our love, our joys, our sorrows, and find our quiet times with God!

I've tried to set it up to be as comfortable and restorative as possible. My nightstand is a small, old oak table with tall legs, covered with a cross-stitched white cloth. It holds a Bible, fresh flowers, and an oil lamp.

The table on my husband Bob's side has a more masculine look with his books, a plant, and often, a pile of magazines. Both of us love to crawl in bed early and spend the evening reading our various materials.

Developing a feel and atmosphere of peacefulness is very important. Spend some effort to make your bedroom a welcoming place. You don't have to be an interior designer. Simply use your own creativity and make it the happiest room in your world. Make your bedroom a sanctuary.

Simple Pleasures

- Memorize a poem that has significance for you and share it.
- Dust your sheets with a talc-free, herbal powder before bed.
- Place a leaf between wax paper, iron it, and put it under your husband's pillow.

Wisdom for Living

Dear Father, may my home reflect the peace You have put in my heart. May it be a place of rest for those I love. A place of rest and of love.

You'll Be Surprised

God, even thy God, hath anointed thee with the oil of gladness above thy fellows.

HEBREWS 1:9 (KJV)

I wasn't surprised. My ideas and my children's ideas about organization were as different as night and day, as far apart as the North Pole from the South! What did surprise me, however, was how willing they were to learn!

I wish that I had realized this sooner. Things would have been a lot easier. By the time they were about 12 years old, I was desperate. I couldn't do it all myself. I knew it was time to delegate, so I started with Jenny.

I gave her a set of colorful file folders and a fun pen and showed her how to set up her own filing system. She had a file for report cards, all her special school reports, photographs, and letters (I'm sure she even had a love letter or two tucked away!). When she got her first car, the insurance papers all went into the file box, and when she filed her first tax return, she created a separate file for that, too.

Gradually, Jenny's room took on a neater, more ordered appearance and it seemed to please her as well. Teach your children about organization. You'll be surprised!

Simple Pleasures

- Fill a cooler with cold drinks when you go on a long car trip.
- Stop to see out-of-town friends.
- Share some simple pleasures with a child.

Wisdom for Living

O God, how different each of us is from the other, and yet, how similar we are. Today, give me patience with the differences and a true appreciation of what they reveal about You.

Rush or Rest?

> *But thou art a God ready to pardon, gracious and merciful, slow to anger, and of great kindness....*
>
> NEHEMIAH 9:17 (KJV)

Whether you have children or not, if you get a late start in the morning you'll be hurrying to catch up all day. Even Benjamin Franklin noted that fact with one of his witty sayings: "He that riseth late must trot all day!" I know that he must have had mothers in mind. So what can we do to help manage the responsibilities and duties of family living? Simply this—delegate!

Delegating isn't easy for anyone. And if you have children, then you have to get up a little earlier to make delegating work for you. It is an important aspect of motherhood.

Tape pictures of socks, T-shirts, and other clothes on dresser drawers. Then your children will know where everything goes when they put their clothing away.

Use my "three-bag system" with all your children: give away, put away, and throw away!

Set a small alarm clock to go off five minutes before it's time to leave for school or before it's time to start their homework. Oven clocks work well for this, too.

Escape rush hour through careful delegating, and then enter into rest!

Simple Pleasures

No man who is in a hurry is quite civilized.

—WILL DURANT

Wisdom for Living

Oh, how I need Your gentle kindness this day to see me through, Lord. Quiet my heart and my mind that I may share the gifts of Your Spirit with those around me.

No Time to Quit

*But we are not of those
back and are destroyed
those who believe and a*

HEB

Has it been one of those days? Are you about ready to toss in the towel—the one you've been picking up all day because no one else seems to bother? Have you ever wanted to quit, but there just doesn't seem to be the time!

Take a deep breath, find a quiet moment, have a cold beverage, and take some time to simply rest!

Thankfully, the Lord is always there to meet with you, waiting to fill your cup with encouragement and affirmation, waiting mercifully to restore your soul. He does it through the words of Scripture and through the soft whisper of His Holy Spirit.

Ironically, He also encourages and affirms us through the very people who never pick up their clothes, who leave the dirty dishes in the sink, and who never put the cap on the toothpaste! These are also the ones who love you, accept you, and support you.

Job 22:23 says, "If you return to the Almighty, you will be restored." How we need that restoration today!

Simple Pleasures

Every morning must start from scratch,
with nothing on the stoves—that is cuisine.

—FERNAND POINT

Wisdom for Living

My simple prayer is this: restore me Lord, and I will be restored.

More Than Lace and Flowers

I will give thanks to Thee, for I am fearfully and wonderfully made; wonderful are Thy works, And my soul knows it very well.

PSALM 139:14 (NASB)

What is better than a good woman? According to the Bible, not much. Proverbs 31 tells us that a gracious and wise woman is worth far more than rubies.

As women of God, we're so much more than lace and flowers! We're called to be women after God's own heart. Women with teachable hearts who can give and forgive, protect and respect. It is possible—we can go from craze to praise. And in so doing, we can become the kind of women whose children and husbands rise up and call us blessed.

How do we build a life filled with this kind of joy? Begin today by praying that God's life will permeate your heart and mind. Pray that your life will flow with His love and His peace, with His Spirit and His joy. It's not just about primping and polishing. We want to take the love of God and wrap it around each task we do, each errand we run, each neighbor we meet today. Our privilege as women of God is to fill our homes with prayer, peace, and pleasure. That's the beautiful gift that comes with the spirit of femininity! Celebrate it today!

Simple Pleasures

The best part of beauty is that which no picture can express.

—FRANCIS BACON

Wisdom for Living

You made me! You did such a wonderful job, Father! Teach me how to care for the body, mind, and soul that You have given me.

November

TRADITIONS TO REMEMBER

Prepare Yourself in the Evening

My soul waiteth for the Lord more than they that watch for the morning.

PSALM 130:6 (KJV)

"Lord, make me a good steward of my time." Is this is your prayer? Here are some practical ways to save time each day!

- Do errands on the way to or from work.
- Delegate jobs and responsibilities to other members of your family.
- Get up one half hour earlier.
- Don't be distracted by the TV. Why not turn it off?
- Cook more than one meal at a time.
- Scratch things off your To Do list that aren't a priority. Learn to say no.

To the ancient Hebrews, each new day began in the evening. Each evening was devoted to rest, to family, and to fellowship—as well as to study and meditate in God's Word. Try devoting some of your time in the evening to quiet reflection and some inner planning. In other words, prepare yourself in the evening for the coming day.

Remember, good things seldom happen by accident.

Simple Pleasures
- Organize old photos.
- Sort out clothing that didn't get worn last summer and give it away.
- Talk together at the dinner table.

Wisdom for Living
I need You, O Lord. I am empty and needy.
Fill me with Your joy and strength this day so that
I might serve You faithfully every hour of every day.

The Beauty of Meal Planning

To every thing there is a season, and a time to every purpose under the heaven.

ECCLESIASTES 3:1 (KJV)

Time is a precious and limited resource. Therefore, all of us need to find ways to be more efficient so that we have time for the things we really enjoy. When we consider that the average woman cooks, plans for, shops for, cleans up after, or goes out to eat more than 750 meals a year, we understand how important it is to keep it simple!

Prepare meals that can be stored in Tupperware or plastic containers in the freezer or refrigerator and then reheated later for quick feasts. To bake potatoes more quickly, simply put a clean nail through the potato. It'll cook in half the time. Do you have leftover pancakes or waffles? Don't toss them—freeze them. Then pop them into the toaster or oven for a quick and easy breakfast or snack. Sandwiches can be made up by the week and frozen. Put on all the ingredients except the lettuce.

Meal planning saves you time, saves you money, saves you stress, and makes for happier meals, happier children, and happier husbands! It takes time to plan ahead, but when you discipline yourself to "just do it," you'll be amazed at how much more time and attention you can give to the important things God has given you to do.

Simple Pleasures

The discovery of a new dish does more for the happiness of mankind than the discovery of a star.

—ANTHELME BRILLAT-SAVARIN

Wisdom for Living

Sometimes I am discouraged by the "dailyness" of life. Calm me today, Father. Help me to set my affections on things above, and to give You thanks.

The Famous "Love Basket"

Remembering without ceasing your work of faith, and labour of love, and patience of hope in our Lord Jesus Christ, in the sight of God and our Father.

1 THESSALONIANS 1:3 (KJV)

Many of you who have read my books and attended my seminars know that I like to find simple ways to say "I love you!"

One of my all-time favorites is the "love baskets." They are the perfect demonstration of the first fruit of the spirit—love! I've been making them for more than 40 years for my friends and family.

One Valentine's Day, Bob and I weren't able to be together for our usual special dinner. The next morning I called him at work and said, "Honey, I'm taking you to a special restaurant that has your favorite food. Could you be home by six o'clock?"

At five-thirty that night, my Bob was coming through the door of our home ready for his evening out with his sweetheart. Little did he know that I had fixed his favorite southern-fried chicken, potato salad, fruit, and a yummy dessert. I set the table beautifully with candles—everything was super-special! It was a "love basket" for my husband! Was he pleased? You bet he was! Try preparing one for someone you love.

Simple Pleasures

* Prepare a glorious seafood quiche brimming with crab and Gruyere cheese.
* Southern-fried chicken with mashed potatoes and creamy gravy is always a favorite.
* Treat your family to a dessert of apple crisp, warm from the oven, with a dollop of cream.

Wisdom for Living

Love is practical, Lord. Thank You for fresh ideas of how I can show my love to those around me. I'm listening for Your voice. I trust You to be my helper.

Selfish or Caring for Yourself?

What shall I render unto the Lord for all his benefits toward me?

PSALM 116:12 (KJV)

As a young mom, I labored from sunup to sundown doing the things that moms do. I was exhausted. After several years I remember saying to myself, "I need some time just for me. I need help!" But for some reason, with all there was to do, I felt selfish even thinking that way.

Then the Lord brought me new understanding. Leviticus 19:18 (NASB) says, "You shall love your neighbor as yourself." What a profound, yet simple principle. I realized that unless I took care of myself, I could never be an authentic caregiver to others.

I started to get up a half hour before everyone else so that I could spend time in the Scriptures over an early cup of coffee or tea. This one activity had an incredible effect on my outlook.

As I found new and creative ways to take a moment to care for myself, I found that I had more energy and care to give to others. Relax in a cozy, warm bath. Have your nails done once in awhile. Listen to a favorite CD. Write a poem. When you spend some time on yourself, you become more relaxed, and your home will function better.

Simple Pleasures

* Display assorted teas aligned in a pretty basket—black, green, or herbal.
* Find a recipe for Russian tea. It's soothing and wonderfully aromatic.
* Store coffee in air-tight containers. Grind as needed and brew fresh.

Wisdom for Living

In solitude is solace. Lord, I seek the quiet of solitude
so that I might hear Your voice more clearly, be prepared
to follow You more nearly, and love You more dearly.

Build Yourself Up

She is clothed with strength and dignity; she can laugh at the days to come. She speaks with wisdom, and faithful instruction is on her tongue.

PROVERBS 31:25-26

Have you ever known a woman who was truly satisfied with herself, with how God made her? I'm not sure I have. There's always something we want to change about the way we look, the way we act, or our abilities. You name it—we want to change it!

The problem with this kind of negative thinking is that it will eventually poison our system. When we concentrate on our imperfections, we have a tendency to look at what's wrong and ignore what's right. We can't be built up when we constantly tear ourselves down. So how do we break away from negative thoughts?

For starters, prepare yourself to work at this. Old thought patterns die hard. It's not going to be easy, so go a little easy on yourself.

Buy yourself a journal if you don't have one already. Write down five negative thoughts you have about yourself. Beside each one, list the positive aspects of those imperfections. Then pray about them and ask God to help you adjust your perspective. Simply bringing your self-image before the Lord is a powerful statement of faith. Acknowledge that you are God's creation, and praise Him!

Simple Pleasures

If religion has done nothing for your temper,
it has done nothing for your soul.

—MATTHEW HENRY

Wisdom for Living

You made me just as I am. I surrender myself to You today, dear Father, and ask You to continue Your creative work in me so that I might be all that You originally intended me to be.

A Family That Worships Together

And they, continuing daily with one accord in the temple, and breaking bread from house to house, did eat their meat with gladness and singleness of heart.

ACTS 2:46 (KJV)

In our fragmented and frantic society, family mealtimes are almost a thing of the past. But when you do gather, whether you are a large family, small family, or maybe just living alone, you can honor the Lord by heeding the example of Jesus and worshiping God as you fellowship around the table.

Matthew 26:26 (NASB) says, "Jesus took some bread, and after a blessing, He...gave it to the disciples and said, 'Take, eat; this is My body.'" One practice any family can maintain is a time of worship whenever the family comes together at mealtimes.

Get together as a family as often as you can. Or invite the neighbors over for soup and sandwiches. When you do, you will understand why our Lord, when He broke bread with His friends, told them that as often as they broke bread together, they should remember Him. "Do this in remembrance of Me" is etched on communion tables all over the world.

It's all about stopping to remember the source of our blessings, and honoring the God we serve. Let's incorporate this practice into our lives as often as we can.

Simple Pleasures

There is nothing l like better than a bowl of hot soup, its wisp of aromatic steam teasing the nostrils into quivering anticipation.

—LOUIS DEGOUY, *THE SOUP BOOK,* 1949

Wisdom for Living

Thank You, Lord, that You are the King of creation and Captain of my soul.

233

We Need Phone Time

I have set watchmen upon thy walls, O Jerusalem, which shall never hold their peace day nor night

ISAIAH 62:6 (KJV)

We are famous for our need to communicate with other women! It's one of our trademarks. If you can't seem to get all your chores done, and you need to find time to visit with a mother, a sister, or a friend, then consider a cordless phone. Or better yet, buy one of those nifty headsets that leaves both hands free while you move about the house. After all, if we're going to make our lives a little less complicated, then we need to learn to do two things at once—especially in the kitchen.

While you're on the phone, you can load or unload the dishwasher, cook a meal, or mop a floor. You can dust your bookshelves, polish silver, or fold clothes. If you have a phone set that works outside, you can water or deadhead your flowers.

Here are some other tips. Prepare foods for your freezer while visiting by phone. Cut fresh bagels in half. When you're ready to use them, they'll defrost faster. Peel apples for a pie, pull together the ingredients for a pumpkin pie, or cut up vegetables for a hearty fall soup.

Be creative! We can't do it all, but we can probably do more, if we plan for it!

Simple Pleasures
The language of friendship is not words, but meanings.

Wisdom for Living
Lord, I don't want to talk just to be talking. Govern my thoughts and my words so that they will glorify Your name. May others desire You because of what they see of You in me.

Children Love Spoon Bread

But may the righteous be glad and rejoice before God; may they be happy and joyful.

Have you ever come up short on fun ideas for children or grandchildren? Here's a simple way to spend time with them and have a fun cooking experience to boot! Not only that, but I also want you to have a great recipe for Quickie Spoon Bread.

Our grandson, Chad, loves making spoon bread, and asks to do it often. He began making this recipe when he was nine years old.

First, you can take your child shopping for the ingredients. You'd be surprised how enjoyable shopping with a child can be if you aren't trying to do 50 things at once.

Here are the ingredients:

1 box of Jiffy corn bread mix
2 cups of creamed corn
1 small can of green chilies (chopped)
1 teaspoon sugar
1 egg

Mix it all well and spoon into a muffin pan (lined with cupcake papers). Bake according to the Jiffy package directions.

Twelve minutes later, you've got Spoon Bread! And what a fun and easy time you will have spent with someone you love!

Simple Pleasures

Had I but one penny in the world,
thou shouldst have it for gingerbread.

—WILLIAM SHAKESPEARE, *LOVE'S LABOUR'S LOST*

Wisdom for Living

I know I need to lighten up. Your life within me calls me to rejoice, to dance, to celebrate before You. I will celebrate. Sing unto the Lord, Sing to the Lord a new song!

The Giveaway Principle

...Having received from Epaphroditus what you have sent, a fragrant aroma, an acceptable sacrifice, well-pleasing to God.

PHILIPPIANS 4:18 (NASB)

As American consumers we face a growing problem—the overcrowding of our homes. Whether we live in an apartment or a six-bedroom home, every closet, cupboard, refrigerator, and garage is crammed with the abundance of our possessions. Some of us have so much that we go out and rent additional storage areas simply because we have too many things for the space we live in!

Bob and I are no different from you. We buy new clothes and cram them into our closets. We purchase a new antique treasure and put it in the corner. I see a beautiful quilt that would really warm up our guest room, and I can't resist. And on and on. Soon, we're closed in with no room to breathe! Life isn't so simple anymore, is it?

Not too long ago, we made a rule in our home that has helped us be good stewards of our abundance. Every time we purchase a new item, we look for something in our home that we can either give away or sell. This commitment has resulted in great some great annual garage sales! And it's a blessing to know that someone else is using what we really don't need anymore. Share with others what you aren't using!

Simple Pleasures

- Give a cherished possession as a birthday gift to someone you love.
- Donate your time to a local charity.
- Say a blessing over your children as they go out the door.

Wisdom for Living

Heavenly Father, grant me the spirit of generosity. May I pour out blessings on others in the same way that You have poured out Your blessings on me.

There's No Place Like Home

I go to prepare a place for you.

JOHN 14:2 (KJV)

How many times have you seen *The Wizard of Oz*? As our children were growing up, it was one of our most beloved family films, and it's annual showing on television was always a much-anticipated event.

Of course, it's Dorothy who wants to leave home, and then realizes after her journey through Oz that "there's no place like home." Maybe today, you can make your house seem a little more like home.

Start by eliminating anything that contributes to squirming, shivering, or squinting! There should always be a comfortable spot for every member of the family. If your budget is limited, this may have to be a long-term goal, but it's an important one!

Create a place where you can comfortably interact with members of your family or close friends. Look for a place that invites members of your family to have a few moments alone, to talk with God, and to be refreshed.

The soft glow of lamplight, a warm rug to wiggle your toes in, cozy afghans to snuggle up in—these things can make your house feel like home!

Simple Pleasures

I'd rather have roses on my table than diamonds on my neck.

—EMMA GOLDMAN

Wisdom for Living

Someday I will be with You, Lord—face-to-face. What a homecoming that will be! Until then, I pray my home can be filled with the love and goodness that comes from heaven.

Simplify, Simplify

Thus says the Lord, "Set your house in order…"

ISAIAH 38:1 (NASB)

Life can be much easier. Does that thought appeal to you today? The key is to learn the wonderful art of simplicity. If we truly learn to *keep it simple*, we will find life much richer and full of more meaningful moments. Here are a few lessons on keeping life simple.

One of the basics is knowing what to throw away. Remember, less is better than more. The bonus: In the long run, you will save a lot of cleaning time!

Before you buy something, ask yourself, "Where am I going to put this?" Make sure that you have a clearly defined place in mind for anything that you buy. If you don't, your priceless treasure could become nothing more than expensive clutter. Be ruthless with your possessions. When in doubt, throw it out! If it doesn't have an appropriate place, then it's just taking up space, and you'll probably spend a lot of time cleaning it and moving it around. It won't bring you the delight you hoped it would.

By simplifying, you make time to do what you want to do and need to do. This will help you make your life what God wants it to be!

Simple Pleasures

- Polish a collection of silver spoons.
- Stack a basket of wood on a hearth in preparation for a cozy time.
- Use a pretty ribbon to suspend an orange covered in cloves.

Wisdom for Living

Lord, Your simplifying hand is upon me. You are bringing order to my life. You are bringing me into a new place of peace and rest.

Generation to Generation

These stones shall become a memorial to the sons of Israel forever.

JOSHUA 4:7 (NASB)

One of the most important reasons for establishing a home is the transmission of values and traditions. Traditions are worth weaving into the fabric of your family's life. The memories and the lessons that come from them are truly important. They are the tools that one generation uses to teach another!

When I'm serving a tea party to my granddaughter and grandsons (which we do often), I'm passing on to them the things my mother passed on to me. Not only do we experience the joy of spending time together, but also, the value of manners and the power of small rituals is transmitted to their hearts and lives forever.

When my husband, Bob, reads Bible stories to our grandchildren or works with them in our garden, he passes along the treasures that his family gave him: a deep faith in God, a love of growing things, and a respect for hard work.

When we all participate together in family gatherings and traditions, when we watch videos, play board games, and enjoy other simple things together, we build a chain of memories that will stretch unbroken into the future. Don't neglect those important moments!

Simple Pleasures

He is happiest, be he king or peasant,
who finds peace in his home.

—GOETHE

Wisdom for Living

*Build up my faith in You, Lord, so that my life can be
a testimony to those around me.*

My Prayer Basket

Do not merely listen to the word, and so deceive yourselves. Do what it says.

JAMES 1:22

I'd like to encourage you to make God's Word the foundation of your security and strength.

As I've practiced the discipline of spending time in God's Word, I've discovered the value of what I call my prayer basket. Over the years, I've gotten in the habit of keeping a prayer basket close at hand. Seeing my basket waiting for me is a wonderful invitation to spend time with my Lord in devotion and prayer.

Just what's in my prayer basket? Well, it contains the things that I've found to help me effectively learn and grow in my relationship with the Lord. I've put in a Bible, a daily devotional, my prayer planner, a journal and pen, and a bouquet of silk flowers to remind me of the beauty and fragrance of the Lord Jesus Himself.

Because I love sharing the strength of my security with others, I also have a small box of tissues handy for my times of fellowship with friends in need. In addition, I've tucked a few pretty postcards or notecards in my basket for those moments when I feel moved to communicate God's love to someone I'm praying for.

Simple Pleasures

Pray to God and row to shore.

—A RUSSIAN PROVERB

Wisdom for Living

Lord, teach me to pray. Lord, move me to prayer. Lord, grace me with the strength and resolve to make talking with You my highest priority.

The Treasure of Tradition

Fix these words of mine in your hearts and minds....Teach them to your children.

DEUTERONOMY 11:18-19

You've seen your little ones do it—they giggle as you play that childhood game of peek-a-boo. You hide your face behind your hands and they giggle with delight. "Again!" they exclaim. And I giggle too, enjoying the moment of discovery, and relishing this very instant when my little granddaughter first begins to celebrate tradition.

At its simplest level, isn't that why traditions are begun? We experience something good and joyful and meaningful—and we want to do it again. And why not? Repeating good experiences is one way we begin to learn and to make sense of our lives.

But there's more. Tradition also helps us understand and celebrate who we are. It teaches us to be thankful for the gift of life, and for the people God used to give it to us.

Proverbs 24:3-4 puts it this way:

By wisdom a house is built,
  and through understanding it is established;
through knowledge its rooms are filled
  with rare and beautiful treasures.
"Again!"

Simple Pleasures

- Children love to watch a father or older brother carve the holiday turkey.
- Hold hands for grace; squeeze the hand you're holding.
- Cranberry sauce served just once a year is a treat!

Wisdom for Living

Father, our confidence is based in Your Word. Your Word is true. Let wisdom reign in my life, dear Lord, as I put my trust in You.

A Child's Room

And the child grew and became strong; he was filled with wisdom, and the grace of God was upon him.

LUKE 2:40

Where do you start when you decorate children's rooms? You start with the children! Unless they are infants, give them a say in what their room will be like. It's a gift that you can give them to create a room that looks just like them!

Children can help decorate their room at a surprisingly young age. Even a toddler can look at a few colors or patterns and pick a favorite.

The more input your children have in the décor of their room, the more responsible they're likely to be in keeping it tidy. (You'll notice I said "likely.")

One child I know stenciled the names of her friends in several colors on one wall. Then she used those same colors in the linens and drapes in the room. Keep it simple, but encourage your children to use their God-given imaginations!

Enjoy this "bedroom" time with them, and use those moments to talk about who they are and why God loves them. Creating their room environment together is a chance to create moments you'll cherish later.

Simple Pleasures

- You can enjoy special moments with your children while you teach them about orderliness.
- Finding a room straightened by a child is very rewarding!
- Watching a child sleep brings stillness and peace to our own hearts.

Wisdom for Living

Thank You, Lord, for the children You have placed in my life. Give me sensitivity to their individual uniqueness. Help me to affirm and support them in their growing lives.

242

Things We Never Thought

Becoming a creative person can be very practical. Being practical means using what you already have and working with it. Here are some simple examples that might spur you on to greater things.

Dig out those old evening bags. They're "decorating gold," as are a lot of other things you've been collecting. What in the world can you do to decorate with evening bags? Hang them as a small grouping on the wall or in a shadow box. They can make a lovely display! And that costume jewelry—hang some of the more interesting pieces on a ribbon of lace and display them in a window or on a wall.

Travel mementos from long ago that lie crammed away in some drawer can be "creatively" retrieved and displayed on shelves or even in a frame.

Line up old books on shelves or stack them on tables. My grandmother had a wonderful collection, always on display. They live on in my memory even today.

Use what you've collected to make your home as inviting and beautiful as possible. Keep it simple! Your decorations don't have to be expensive or complicated.

Simple Pleasures

* Toast crumpets, add marmalade, and serve them at four o'clock with tea.
* Purchase a walking stick in an antique store.
* Enjoy your favorite TV program together while eating on dinner trays.

Wisdom for Living

Thank You, dear Lord, for grandparents, aunts, and uncles whose investment in my life has made such a difference. Bless their memory today. May their legacy be a source of strength in my life.

My Gift Shelf

Fear not, little flock; for it is your Father's good pleasure to give you the kingdom.

LUKE 12:32 (KJV)

I just love my gift shelf! Every home should have one! Here are some ideas for a special gift shelf in your home!

Begin by thinking ahead and being on the lookout year 'round for items that will be useful or that will make a thoughtful gift. You can begin by picking up a few nice items—a box of stationery, a little teddy bear, or a pretty candleholder.

When it's time for a birthday party gift or hospitality gift, visit your gift shelf and see what treasures have accumulated there. If you've been diligent over the months, you will probably have something just right. And there is an added bonus—you probably purchased that item when it was on sale, without the pressure of last-minute buying, so you've probably saved some expense as well!

Here is another helpful hint: make sure you also have a gift wrap spot set aside. Store your wrapping paper with colored ribbon, scotch tape, and some dried or silk flowers for decoration. Have some nice cards you can use with your gift.

Preserve the joy of gift-giving with this simple idea—the gift shelf!

Simple Pleasures

- Buy quality gift wrap from a child and support school fund-raising.
- Begin a gift record—you'll never worry about giving the same gift twice.
- Team up with a relative or friend on a gift—you'll be able to afford something a little nicer than what you might have given on your own.

Wisdom for Living

I am the recipient of such abundance and blessing!
Where can I give today, Lord?

A Festive Friday Night

> But exhort one another daily,
> while it is called To day; lest any
> of you be hardened through the
> deceitfulness of sin.
>
> HEBREWS 3:13 (KJV)

At the end of a busy week, there's nothing like a Friday night with "white space on the calendar." Those nights are rare, but the last time it happened, I decided to quickly put together a "love basket" to surprise my Bob.

I grabbed my trusty basket with the sturdy handle and lined it with a patterned tablecloth about 45 inches square. It looked elegant hanging over the sides. Inside, I put two stemmed glasses with two cloth napkins tucked in each glass. Fluffing up the napkins at the top of the glasses added a nice touch.

I needed to set the mood, so I added a tall candleholder, candle, a bottle of sparkling cider, a loaf of French bread, and plenty of fresh flowers. Some of Bob's favorite foods were left over in the refrigerator, so I put those in as well. I was ready—all I needed was a quiet spot.

What an evening! Moments to remember aren't difficult to create. Just remember to keep it simple and you'll be fine. After all, the simple things make life enjoyable!

Simple Pleasures

- Browse through catalogs and anticipate the spring.
- Have a spa day and treat yourself to a massage and facial.
- Pour out your love on someone special.

Wisdom for Living

I love how much You love a heart that desires to please You!
Today, in little things and big, may I please You.

Home Sweet Home

Here I am! I stand at the door and knock. If anyone hears my voice and opens the door, I will go in and eat with him, and he with me.

REVELATION 3:20

Your home can be a place of refuge, a place you and others enjoy coming to. Does that seem impossible? If you live in a house with small children, you're already shaking your head. "Emilie, I have to *leave* home to get way from all the noise and turmoil! It's never quiet at my house."

Let's be a little creative and see what we can do about that. See what happens in your home when you put on some soothing music. Even pets respond to melodious sounds.

Take a few moments to place something bright or pretty near the door to greet your family or guests. Before your husband, children, or roommates arrive home, light a few scented candles, get some spices boiling on the stove, or—most powerful of all—fill your home with the aroma of dinner in the oven!

As we open our hearts and minds to God, putting Him first in our lives, He will show us little ways to organize the chaos in our lives and live more simply and peacefully. Believe me, it's worth all the effort you put into it. A peaceful home truly glorifies the Lord.

Simple Pleasures

- Install a new screen door that closes quietly.
- Make enough room in your garage for your car.
- Aren't you glad when all the leaves are finally off the trees?

Wisdom for Living

Peace, Lord. I need Your peace for myself, and I want to give Your peace to others today! I love You, Father.

Old-fashioned Simplicity

I am the bread of life.

JOHN 6:48

Have you ever wondered how the homemakers of yesteryear made their kitchens into an inviting place where everyone felt welcome? They didn't have a lot of fancy fabrics or elaborate kitchen appliances to create something special. Instead, they did it the old-fashioned way—simply.

Placing a bowl of freshly washed lemons on the table is a great way to say hello. After baking an apple pie, set it on the counter to cool—and perfume the house. Pile some fresh apples next to it for a delightful "before and after" look.

Hang a basket—or 30 baskets—from the ceiling beam.

Freeze grapes and roll them in granulated sugar. Store them in a glass bowl or on a pretty plate, and toss them in a salad or use them as a garnish.

Next time you make buttered toast, sprinkle some cinnamon and sugar on it. It's an old idea, but when was the last time you made cinnamon toast?

Take time today to smell the roses—and the soup! Remember, it doesn't have to be modern to be meaningful. Some of the most special traditions are those that simply show good, old-fashioned love and hospitality.

How about some cinnamon toast with a cup of tea right now?

Simple Pleasures

"My desire," wrote William Wordsworth of
Dove Cottage, "is to sit without emotion, hope,
or aim in the loved presence of my cottage fire."

Wisdom for Living

*O God, You are the source of my life. Feed me with
the joy of Your Spirit; nourish me with the meat of Your Word.
Let my life be a provision for others.*

A Friend Indeed

True friendship is a rare commodity. Use your creativity today to reach out to someone in need.

When our daughter's friend began her battle with cancer, we had a luncheon for her before her bone marrow transplant. Five of us enjoyed eating Cobb salads and croissants, topping off our meal with yogurt and fresh fruit parfaits. But we weren't finished yet! The best part was still to come!

Each of us got a colored marking pen and a sheet of paper and traced Lynn's hand on it. Then we each added a small heart in the outlined hand.

Once our "Lynn hand" was complete, we placed one hand on Lynn's hand and one hand on our paper hand and prayed for her healing and her future.

As we returned to our homes that day, we pasted our copies of Lynn's handprint on our refrigerator doors. Every time we passed the frig, we placed our hand in Lynn's and prayed for her.

We experienced God's loving hand on Lynn's life, and on our own, as we helped support our friend through a time of crisis.

Simple Pleasures

If you have knowledge, let others light their candles at it.

—ANONYMOUS

Wisdom for Living

You hold the power of life and death, Father.
Strengthen me this day by Your Holy Spirit.

December

CELEBRATING THE MOMENT

Worth a Thousand Words

...Be ready always to give an answer to every man that asketh you a reason of the hope that is in you with meekness and fear.

1 PETER 3:15 (KJV)

The pictures we hang on our walls reveal a lot about who we are. They are expressions of that which pleases or delights us. Often they tell others who or what matters most in our lives. For that reason, you don't have to limit yourself to traditional forms of art when you are choosing wall decorations. Anything from a trivet to a tray will do. In fact, an arrangement of objects with varying shapes and sizes can be very effective. Whenever you find an empty wall, consider it an opportunity to make your home more interesting and inviting!

In the same way, that which we choose to give our time to and talk about also expresses that which we hold dear and the things that really matter in our lives. Isaiah 52:13 (NASB) says,

Behold, My servant will prosper,
He will be high and lifted up, and greatly exalted.

As you go through this day, hold up the Lord Jesus Christ in all you do. Let the eyes of your heart focus on Him. As you do, your words and everything else in your life will reflect His goodness and His love. That's the perfect picture! It's the picture of our Lord Jesus Christ.

Simple Pleasures

* Warm your home with plaid blankets, throws, pillows, or pottery.
* Tie a ribbon on every vase and bring the outdoors in.
* An evergreen bough laced with pine cones or berries is simplicity itself.

Wisdom for Living

Lord, help me to evaluate what really matters to me.
I want my life to reflect eternal values and kingdom priorities.
Bring Your understanding to me today.

Moment by Moment

Did you know that the average American spends 27 hours a year at red lights? If that's really the case, then shouldn't we plan to use those 27 hours in some productive way?

While you're sitting there, listen to a book on tape, or enjoy one of your favorite Christian programs in the radio. Keep your prayer journal with you and lift up a friend or family member in prayer. Quickly review your grocery list to make sure nothing is forgotten. Think of ideas for your niece or nephew's upcoming birthday. Consider how you might rearrange your flower bed once fall arrives.

Remember that you are the master of your life and of your time. Carry a small tape recorder with you to record a message while you wait, or use it to practice a verse you are memorizing.

We all know we waste time when we try to do too much all at once. But using those blank moments in the day can make help you to accomplish some of the things you have on your mind.

Simple Pleasures

Oh! For a book, and a cozy nook
And oh! For a quiet hour…

—ANONYMOUS

Wisdom for Living

Every moment, at every red light, I wait on You, Lord.
May I never be ashamed. I trust in You.

Top Time-Wasters

> But you, dear friends, build yourselves up in your most holy faith and pray in the Holy Spirit.
>
> JUDE 1:20

"In quietness and confidence shall be your strength. In returning and rest shall be your salvation." Here are five time-wasters that keep us from the "returning and rest" that we need.

1. Trying to do too much at once. Learn to prioritize your tasks.
2. Failing to plan. Successful time managers make a plan and set priorities.
3. Inability to say no. Maintain a balance of personal, family, and work time.
4. Putting things off. Don't waste time agonizing over an unpleasant chore—either do it right away, hire someone to do it, or forget it.
5. Doing everything yourself. Learn to delegate certain tasks. You can't do it all.

Now make yourself a quick cup of tea, take out your notebook and Bible, and read a favorite passage of Scripture! Let your heart and mind rest in the confidence that the Lord orders the steps of the righteous. Let Him restore your soul today.

Simple Pleasures

- Rediscover the lost art of letter writing—it's a balm to a friendship.
- Pull out the old flannel nightgown and feel cozy all over again.
- A bar cleanser and cool water are still the essence of a beauty ritual.

Wisdom for Living

The enemy wants to discourage me at every turn.
I feel overwhelmed. Lord, help me to set my mind on You.
I need Your grace to trust. You are my King and my God.

The Challenge of Raising Children

He commanded our forefathers to teach their children, so the next generation would know them...then they would put their trust in God.

PSALM 78:5, 7

It's not easy to raise children in today's complicated world. The energy that is required can make us hesitate to have children, or maybe cause us to wish we never had them.

But the Bible tells us that children are a gift from God, and that the man or woman who has them has been blessed indeed. God has given us no greater calling than to be a responsible mother or father. As parents, grandparents, or extended family, we need to be encouragers for our children.

Encourage a child today. Children's little faces light up when they are given recognition for doing something good.

If you don't know a child well enough to be an encourager, then you can encourage his or her parents. You never know the burden you might be lifting by telling a mom or dad that you notice the great effort they put into being a good parent! We all need to hear the words, "Well done."

Your words of encouragement can make a difference in the challenge of raising children.

Simple Pleasures

- Tuck a child into bed and share a story that will appeal to a young dreamer.
- Massage a child's toes and feet to insure peaceful sleep.
- Give a cup of chamomile tea to older children.

Wisdom for Living

Your blessings are countless. Give me boldness to tell others about Your great work in my life.

Little Children Come to Me

I tell you the truth, unless you change and become like little children, you will never enter the kingdom of heaven.

MATTHEW 18:3

What an awesome responsibility it is to bring a precious child into a full understanding of what Jesus did on the cross for him or her. Jesus said, "Let the little children come to me, and do not hinder them, for the kingdom of Heaven belongs to such as these" (Matthew 19:14). How can we possibly keep it simple when it comes to teaching a child what it means to be a child of God? Here are a few simple principles.

Remember that your child belongs primarily to God. When you teach your child how to complete a job, train them step-by-step, with patience. Help them to understand that God has given them abilities and gifts to be used for His glory. Don't assume that the task will be completely learned by watching. Check the results of their work and compliment them. Never redo a chore that a child has just completed. If it can be done better, try again later, and work to communicate on the child's level.

Teach your child what it means to respond to the gifts of God. Show them through your love that God welcomes them into His presence. Don't hinder them. Jesus is inviting them to come. Your love can make a difference.

Simple Pleasures
- Make a Christmas guest book. Let your children offer it to guests.
- Have sparkling cider with your meal tonight. Toast the holidays.
- Cuddle by a cozy fire and plan your Christmas lists and shopping trips.

Wisdom for Living
Lord, I need a childlike heart. Strip me of the defenses and excuses I have built up over the years, and let me enter into Your presence with a humble heart.

254

Teaching Moments

As parents and grandparents, we need to stay alert to recognize opportunities to teach our children about God. We teach children whenever we spend time with them, whenever we are just "being family"!

According to the most recent studies on drug abuse among teens, there are three cornerstones in the lives of young people who *don't* use drugs: religious beliefs, family relationships, and high self-esteem. At any age, your children will be influenced far more by what you practice than by what you preach.

Establish a "work before play" rule at your home. Encourage children to care for their own belongings. Teach your children to write thank you notes. And remember, there are no quick fixes in training children to become responsible. It takes a strong commitment by all concerned, and it takes time!

Today, take a moment to listen to your heavenly Father. We are His children and He wants to teach us how to live. Look for the teaching moment. Maybe He has an adjustment that He wants you to make in order to be more like Him!

Simple Pleasures

Life is like music; it must be composed by ear,
feeling, and instinct, not just by rule.

—SAMUEL BUTLER

Wisdom for Living

Speak to me Lord; I am listening.

A Spiritual Center

For whosoever shall give you a cup of water to drink in my name, because ye belong to Christ, verily I say unto you, he shall not lose his reward.

MARK 9:41 (KJV)

We all need a spiritual center. We need a place where we belong. This spiritual center is something that we experience on the inside, but it is very helpful to have a physical place where we can be reminded about what is really important in life. We need a home.

Home is as much a state of the heart and spirit as it is a specific place. Just as our spirits require physical bodies to do God's work here on earth, most of us need a physical place where we can be refreshed and restored. This place where we meet with God is called home. It doesn't have to be fancy or exotic. Creating a spiritual home doesn't take a lot of money, or even a lot of time. What it does require is a caring and willing spirit. It requires confidence to believe that God will show you how you can care for your physical and spiritual needs.

How will you know when you've created a place that's truly home to your spirit? You'll sense God's presence there. You'll know in your spirit that you are welcoming Him and that He is there with His arms open toward you.

Simple Pleasures

- Listen—the snow is falling.
- Listen—the wind is blowing.
- Listen—God's Spirit is speaking just now.

Wisdom for Living

I come to You today, Lord, to tell You that I love You above all else in my life. I worship Your holiness, and I want to live in Your presence all the day.

Mistakes and Memories

We all love to have things go perfectly. The perfect centerpiece, the perfectly timed meal. "Your food was just perfect!"

But we all know the harsh reality—things are rarely perfect. Someone once said, "A home needs not only candles and confetti to make it joyful—a home also needs connection!" Sometimes, a mistake provides just the right connection!

One family I know turned a birthday cake disaster—one layer sliding off the other before it could even be frosted—into an occasion for laughter. They just frosted the cake as it was and enjoyed it. After that, the tradition remained—something always had to be wrong with the cake. A perfect cake would have been a disappointment!

We can't always plan how or when mistakes will happen, but we can't let that stand in the way of celebrating our families' events. In addition, responding to the unplanned mistakes of life positively will go miles toward teaching your children to handle their own. Make mistakes into memories!

Simple Pleasures

We can read poetry, and recite poetry,
but to *live* poetry—is the symphony of life.

— S. FRANCES FOOTE

Wisdom for Living

*Dear Lord, thank You for the grace that is growing in my life,
helping me to move with Your Spirit, and enabling me to follow
You as You direct my paths.*

A Childhood to Remember

Those things which are revealed belong unto us and to our children for ever.

DEUTERONOMY 29:29 (KJV)

Do you remember your childhood years? Some of us have very pleasant, carefree memories of growing up, while others of us might say that those years were filled with confusion and pain.

If you want to have a ministry to the children in your life, it can begin with remembering what it's like to be a child, and what children like.

Children love to pretend, to imagine, and to create. They love being able to have adventures within safe limits. And every child loves toys!

My friend Anne remembers an old washstand on her grandmother's screened porch that always held a set of blocks, some crayons, and pick-up sticks. The grandchildren always knew where to go for those games. Now Anne's daughter, Elizabeth, and her little cousins also know the secret of the toys on Great-Grandma's porch.

What's the point of telling you this? Simply that the little touches and the care that you show to the children in your life are important ways to share God's love.

Simple Pleasures

Who has not found the Heaven below
Will fail of it above
For Angels rent the House next ours,
Wherever we remove.

—EMILY DICKINSON

Wisdom for Living

Father, I am Your child and Your care for me is the foundation of my life. May I extend that care to others, especially to the children in my life.

A Reason to Celebrate

Now the dwelling of God is with men, and he will live with them.

REVELATION 21:3

"Let's party," goes the familiar phrase. And to that I say, "Amen!"

Proverbs 17:22 says that "a cheerful heart is good medicine." There is much to laugh about. Treasure that laughter. It's time to stop taking ourselves so seriously!

At age seven, our granddaughter, Christine, called her Papa to tell him a joke. That began a long ritual between the two of them of telling each other jokes. In fact, they each bought a joke book and are still passing funny stories back and forth! Their joy of simple humor makes the rest of us smile, too.

Cultivate the spirit of celebration in your life by making room for laughter. Deliberately seek it out! Begin today as you smile at someone and find something worth laughing about.

You'll be surprised at the way the spirit of celebration will take root in your heart, and you'll rediscover the meaning of another Proverb: "A cheerful heart has a continual feast" (Proverbs 15:15).

Simple Pleasures

- Lay your plans for the New Year.
- Spend a night away from home after the holidays. Take time to restore and renew.
- Gather friends and carol in the neighborhood. Serve hot cider afterward.

Wisdom for Living

*I will celebrate,
sing unto the Lord,
sing to the Lord a new song.*

Christmas Can Be Practical

> On coming to the house, they saw the child with his mother Mary, and they bowed down and worshiped him.
>
> MATTHEW 2:11

I love Christmas! The colors, the music, the special church pageants, the decorations—all of it!

Here are some simple suggestions for unique, homemade, holiday gifts:

- Make a batch of bran muffins. Give away the recipe and the baking tin—with six fresh muffins still inside. Wrap it with cellophane and a pretty bow. Muffin lovers will be delighted!
- How about a favorite recipe tucked in a basket with one or two of the main ingredients.
- Cover shoe boxes with wrapping paper and use them as gift boxes. Fill them with stationery items—small scissors, paper clips, marking pens, and thank you notes. Any mom, dad, grandparent, or teacher will love them!
- Cover a box with road maps and fill it with more road maps, a first-aid kit, a teaching tape, or favorite music—anything associated with travel or a car.

Remember, it's the thought that counts! There's no better time than Christmas to express the meaning of God's gift of eternal life. Express it today!

Simple Pleasures

- Hold a decorating party. Decorate gifts, trees, mantels, doors, and windows.
- Paint your door red for the holidays!
- Send money to an orphanage.

Wisdom for Living

Lord, give me the gift of giving this season.
Teach me how to give as You gave, freely and from the heart.
May my gifts be a blessing to others and to You.

The Joy of Giving

> For I say, through the grace given unto me...think soberly, according as God hath dealt to every man the measure of faith.
>
> ROMANS 12:3 (KJV)

I love giving presents. And giving unexpected presents at Christmas captures the true spirit of the season.

I try and give a little something to anyone who has helped me throughout the year, from our newspaper carrier to the seldom-seen dentist! I love to share my thanks with a surprise.

I ask my family to make wish lists for Christmas in November, and they are quite happy to help me. I have all sorts of ideas in mind by the last week of November. I love having time to mull over gift ideas before I begin shopping.

I usually finish my shopping by the second week of December, and then focus on homemade gifts and baskets the following week.

Keep it simple! The love you put into each gift will be what lasts. Christmas is a time for celebrating God's love for us, a time for warmth, fellowship, shared experiences, and hospitality.

Show your heart to those around you this Christmas through simple gift giving.

Simple Pleasures

Merry Old Christmas,...
Heart-touching,
Joy-bringing Christmas,
Day of Grand Memories.

—WASHINGTON IRVING

Wisdom for Living

Heavenly Father, what would I do without Your grace in my life?
Make me a vessel of Your grace and mercy in our hurting world.
Only You can set us free.

Christmas Means Belonging

Anyone who gives you a cup of water in my name because you belong to Christ will certainly not lose his reward.

MARK 9:41

This Christmas, give the gift of belonging. Do some simple things that will show those you love how important they are in your life!

I love to use candles. For me, no decoration is so simple yet so effective in setting a Christmas mood. Here are a couple of hints for you if you decide to use a lot of candles:

* Keep candles in the freezer! If you do, they won't tend to drip or spark when lit.
* If your candles won't stand up, then twist a rubber band around the base before you insert the candle into the holder.

Enjoy Christmas with your family and friends. I love what Dr. James Dobson says about this favorite time of the year: "The great value of traditions comes as you give a family a sense of identity, a belongingness."

When we keep it simple, we can enjoy the holidays and put the emphasis where it belongs—celebrating the birth of the Savior.

Simple Pleasures

* String popcorn and cranberries while Christmas carols play.
* Find a recipe for an English plum pudding and start a new tradition.
* Buy one new Christmas sweater for holiday open houses.

Wisdom for Living

By Your grace, Lord, show me how I can extend Your mercy and grace to those around me. Help me to show the love and acceptance that is available at Your throne.

Keep the Joy

How lovely on the mountains are the feet of him Who brings good news, who announces peace and brings good news of happiness...

ISAIAH 52:7 (NASB)

If you're beginning to feel overwhelmed with all the holiday happenings, then join the club! I've come to believe that it's part of the season ritual. There is almost no way to escape it. Sure, we can plan ahead a little more, but even then, how do we keep our hearts and minds at peace in all the busyness of the holidays?

The answer is this—you're going to need time for yourself if you're going to enjoy the next couple of weeks. Start by giving yourself permission to say no!

These busy days are the perfect time to pamper yourself a bit. Schedule time for a mid-December hair appointment—maybe even a manicure. Do whatever your time and finances will allow, but be sure to rejuvenate yourself. Try to get plenty of sleep and exercise.

Isn't it amazing how often we celebrate Christmas—the joy of the birth of Jesus—by nagging, frustration, and general mayhem in our families?

Take a break. Make life a bit more simple, and spend some quiet time refreshing your body, soul, and spirit.

Simple Pleasures

- Wear red stripes, red checks, and red paisley prints—red, red, red.
- Place mistletoe over at least two doors.
- Float white candles in a glass bowl filled with berries.

Wisdom for Living

You reign, O God! Amidst the hustle and bustle of this season, help me to be a peacemaker, Jesus—someone who comes bringing peace and joy to an often-weary world.

A Nifty Invention

> But if we walk in the light, as he is in the light, we have fellowship with one another, and the blood of Jesus, his Son, purifies us from all sin.
>
> 1 JOHN 1:7

Whoever it was that first came up with the idea of a cookie exchange must have been a genius! Have you enjoyed this wonderful, time-saving novelty yet? If not, ask around and see if you can't finagle an invitation to a cookie exchange party. It's one of the things that has helped keep me sane during the holidays. My first party was so much fun that it's become a necessary part of my Christmas tradition.

I received an invitation one day in December to a cookie exchange. The invitation instructed me to bring seven dozen of my favorite Christmas cookies, along with the recipe written on a card. The following Saturday, I arrived at the party with my cookie offering in hand. What a fun time we had!

We drank Christmas tea, traded cookies, and copied the other recipes on pretty cards provided by our hostess. Then we each received a paper tote bag to take our wonderful collection of goodies home. I came home with seven dozen assorted cookies. My baking time had been cut down from several days to several hours.

In the end, it wasn't just about cookies. It was a time of sweet fellowship, too!

Simple Pleasures

- Read the new classic, *A Cup of Christmas Tea*.
- Reminisce of happy days gone by.
- Rediscover a family tradition that you've been missing.

Wisdom for Living

Thank You, God, for friends. What gifts they are to me,
and what sweet fellowship is ours! Let me be a blessing to my friends.

Make the Holidays Special

His name will be called Wonderful Counselor, Mighty God, Eternal Father, Prince of Peace.

ISAIAH 9:6 (NASB)

It doesn't take much effort to make ordinary things a little more special. Here are a few simple things you can do for the children in your life.

The advent calendar is a wonderful tradition that you can start with your children or grandchildren. Each day a little door on the calendar is opened, symbolizing the coming of Christmas and its significance. Our children used to take turns opening a door each morning at the breakfast table. It was always a moment of simple wonder.

Another special family tradition for us was the annual Christmas photo. As the children got older, it became one of the few times we were all together over the holidays. Be creative—include the pets, teddy bears, and favorite toys. Coordinate your clothing to make it even more fun. Some of the photos we have of past Christmases delight our grandchildren because their parents are hugging dolls and teddy bears!

These times together are wonderful occasions to remind your children of your love and of the love of the Savior we're celebrating.

Simple Pleasures

* Share Christmas secrets.
* Plan Christmas surprises.
* Smile, and laugh, and think of all good things.

Wisdom for Living

Wonderful Counselor, Prince of Peace, anoint me with the gift of a listening heart and mind, that I might hear You and provide a listening ear for others.

The True Spirit of Christmas

Then he put the man on his own donkey, took him to an inn and took care of him.

LUKE 10:34

Each year, Bob and I give some thought to what we can do as an expression of the true meaning of Christmas. There are many wonderful opportunities to reach out at Christmastime.

One of the holiday activities that we have enjoyed the most is temporarily adopting a family. We try to help them with holiday food and gifts. And it seems there's always a chance to tell them about Jesus along the way.

Chuck Colson's Prison Fellowship Ministry has a program called Angel Tree where you can choose the name of a prisoner's child and provide a gift. Giving toys to children in your community through the Toys for Tots program is another avenue to explore.

Sign up through your church to feed the homeless. In the past, this has been an enjoyable undertaking for our church family as well as our own family. As we help those less fortunate, it reminds us of the tremendous blessings we have to share.

Give of yourself during this Christmastime, and continue to give throughout the year.

Simple Pleasures

Out of the bosom of the air,
Out of the cloudfolds of her garment shaken,…
Over the harvest fields forsaken,
Silent, and soft, and slow
Descends the snow.

—HENRY WADSWORTH LONGFELLOW, "SNOW"

Wisdom for Living

I need Your sensitivity this Christmas season. Help me to sort through all the opportunities and needs, and to follow where You lead me today.

Simple Traditions Are Best

> How much more will your Father in heaven give the Holy Spirit to those who ask him!
>
> LUKE 11:13

Christmas traditions don't have to be expensive! They simply need to have special meaning for you and your loved ones. Here are a few things that you and your family can do together to create some memories and traditions that you can pass along to your children and your grandchildren.

- Go caroling in the neighborhood or at a convalescent home.
- Bake Christmas cookies for your child's class at school.
- Enjoy the holiday lights in your hometown, or take a nighttime walk around your neighborhood. It's fun to see all the colorful decorations!
- Have a special hot chocolate time using favorite Christmas mugs.
- Wrap gifts together. Let your children create their own packages.
- Attend your church Christmas programs together. Introduce your children to the music of Handel's *Messiah*. Let them hear it sung, and explain the significance of the words to them.

Christmas traditions don't have to be expensive—just traditional!

Simple Pleasures

- Take a child to see the decorated store windows in a large city.
- Stop for hot chocolate afterwards and listen for the music.
- Give a small gift to add to the memory of a wonderful day.

Wisdom for Living

Oh, how I love these holidays, Lord—these holy days when we celebrate You and Your life on this earth. May all our traditions have their source in Your love and goodness toward us.

The Night Before Christmas

And there were shepherds living out in the fields nearby, keeping watch over their flocks at night.

Oh, I love the night before Christmas. All the presents are wrapped and under the tree, and a certain magic settles over the house in anticipation of Christmas day.

Here are a few ideas to inspire new traditions for a wonderful Christmas Eve and Christmas day:

- Before bedtime, hide new pajamas for each family member in their bedrooms. Let everyone find their PJs, and then gather together to hang the stockings. New pajamas make for nice pictures on Christmas morning, too!
- Gather everyone around the fireplace and read the Christmas story from the Bible, or plan to attend the Christmas Eve service at your church.
- On Christmas morning, start the gift giving with a Christmas carol, or have everyone share a special memory.
- Leave an empty chair at your Christmas table to signify that Jesus is welcome. It's a wonderful way to honor Him.
- After dinner, go for a drive and enjoy the Christmas lights one more time!

Simple Pleasures

- Pray with your spouse.
- Pray with the children in your life.
- Pray with a small group of friends for family health and happiness.

Wisdom for Living

The warmth and joy of the holidays are such a blessing.
May You be foremost in my thoughts this day, Lord, as I enter into all the wonderful festivities of this season.

The Silent Night

Have you ever heard the story of that wonderful Christmas carol, "Silent Night?" It holds a remarkable lesson about God's grace.

On December 23, 1818, in the village of Oberndorf, Austria, church organist Franz Gruber and pastor Mohr discovered a mouse hole in the leather bellows of the church organ. They knew immediately that this meant that the church would be without music at the traditional Christmas Eve service the next night.

Franz shyly gave the pastor a small poem that he had written and asked him to set the poem to music. Pastor Mohr strummed his guitar and came up with a tune to fit the very special words of this new song for the children's choir to perform.

That afternoon, he and Franz Gruber gathered the 12 little boys and girls to rehearse the simple song. That night, the children sang the verses to "Silent Night" with clear voices, and it's been sung around the world ever since.

A hole in the organ bellows seemed like a calamity. But without that hole, a beloved carol would never have been born.

Simple Pleasures

- Sing a Christmas carol every night during December.
- Visit a local living nativity scene as a family.
- Discuss the true meaning of Christmas.

Wisdom for Living

Silence. It is hard to find a quiet moment right now,
but I so need to be before You, Lord, in solitude and silence.
Grant me grace to pause and listen to Your truth
as the shepherds did so long ago on that holy, silent night.

Memories to Cherish

This is my body given for you; do this in remembrance of me.

It's important to find easy ways to capture our family memories. One that works well is to put together a Christmas Memory Book!

To begin this tradition, start with a photo album. Each year, place your family picture on one page and that year's Christmas card on the facing page. Then, simply add some notes about the Christmas festivities and traditions you enjoyed. I always asked our children to add their memories as well.

Christmastime is also a great occasion to watch old family movies. Set aside an evening between Christmas and New Year's to do just that.

After the Christmas holidays, take all the Christmas cards you received and, before or after meals, have each member of the family draw out a card. Read who it was from, and then pray for that person or family. That's a tradition that can last well into the new year.

Keep it simple, and enjoy Christmas with all your heart!

Simple Pleasures

- Look back at new memories.
- Look forward to those that are still to come.
- Thank God for everything that touched your life this year.

Wisdom for Living

Thank You for another Christmastime. Another year has just about come and gone. You have been with me through it all. Thank You, Lord, for Your presence.

Other Books
by Emilie Barnes

❧

Abundance of the Heart

❧

Emilie's Creative Home Organizer

❧

The Heart of Loveliness

❧

Help Me Trust You, Lord

❧

Minute Meditations for Women

❧

More Hours in My Day

❧

Survival for Busy Women

❧